Beyond Rebellion and Exoticism

Tamara Alvarez-Detrell and Michael G. Paulson
General Editors

Vol. 31

The Caribbean Studies series is part of the Peter Lang Humanities list.
Every volume is peer reviewed and meets
the highest quality standards for content and production.

Wedsly Turenne Guerrier

Beyond Rebellion and Exoticism

Selected Visions of Haiti 1892–1994

PETER LANG
New York · Berlin · Bruxelles · Chennai · Lausanne · Oxford

Bibliographic information published by the Deutsche Nationalbibliothek
The Deutsche Nationalbibliothek lists this publication in the Deutsche Nationalbibliografie; detailed bibliographic data is available online at http://dnb.d-nb.de.

Library of Congress Cataloging-in-Publication Data
Names: Guerrier, Wedsly Turenne, author.
Title: Beyond rebellion and exoticism : selected visions of Haiti 1892-1994 / Wedsly Turenne Guerrier.
Description: United States of America : Peter Lang, 2025. | Series: Caribbean studies, 1098-4186 ; vol. 31 | Includes bibliographical references and index.
Identifiers: LCCN 2025008947 (print) | LCCN 2025008948 (ebook) | ISBN 9783034354622 (paperback) | ISBN 9783034354639 (ebook) | ISBN 9783034354646 (epub)
Subjects: LCSH: Haitian literature--History and criticism. | Haiti--In literature. | LCGFT: Literary criticism.
Classification: LCC PQ3948.5.H2 G84 2025 (print) | LCC PQ3948.5.H2 (ebook) | DDC 840.9/972940904--dc23/eng/20250508
LC record available at https://lccn.loc.gov/2025008947
LC ebook record available at https://lccn.loc.gov/2025008948

ISSN 1098-4186
ISBN 978-3-0343-5462-2 (Print)
ISBN 978-3-0343-5463-9 (ePDF)
ISBN 978-3-0343-5464-6 (ePUB)
DOI 10.3726/b22920

© 2025 Peter Lang Group AG, Lausanne (Switzerland)
Published by Peter Lang Publishing Inc., New York (USA)

info@peterlang.com

All rights reserved.
All parts of this publication are protected by copyright.
Any utilization outside the strict limits of the copyright law, without the permission of the publisher, is forbidden and liable to prosecution. This applies in particular to reproductions, translations, microfilming, and storage and processing in electronic retrieval systems.
This publication has been peer reviewed.

www.peterlang.com

*This book is dedicated to the Guerrier family
Especially my nieces and nephews
Serena Carlin, Jamarah Shammah Guerrier, Abbygaëlle Marthe Guerrier
Amhine Belonie Guerrier, Everly Ara Rose Guerrier, Elora Peregrine Guerrier
Abed-Nedjah Desty, Abenadaï Desty, Abijah Desty,
Windsley Edler Guerrier, Jayden Edler Guerrier*

Rise up damned of the earth
Rise up prisoners of starvation
—Jacques Roumain

Table of Contents

Acknowledgments ... 13

Introduction ... 15

Chapter 1   Massillon Coicou: A Reflection on Slavery and Christianity ... 21

Chapter 2   The Notion of Power in *The Tragedy of King Christophe* of Aimé Césaire ... 33

Chapter 3   The Esthetics of Protest: Jacques Roumain's Literary Indictment of the American Occupation of Haiti and the Haitian Catholic Church ... 45

Chapter 4   The Representation of Women's Incarceration During the Duvalier Regimes: Anne-Christine d'Adesky's Feminist Perspective in *Under the Bone* ... 77

Chapter 5   Jean-Claude Martineau: Songs as Cautionary Tales ... 91

Chapter 6   Time for Action: "*Manman, pa ban m tete ankò*" (Mother, stop breastfeeding me) ... 109

Conclusion ... 123

Index ... 127

Wedsly Turenne Guerrier PhD

Acknowledgments

I deeply appreciate the opportunity that the authors Anne-Christine D'Adesky, Emmanuel W. Védrine, and Jean-Claude Martineau provided me with to interview them for this book. These interviews help to furnish crucial information about their lives and their works that the readers will really enjoy.

I am additionally indebted to Dr. Lewis Ampidu Clorméus and Dr. Francois Pierre-Louis for reviewing and writing the endorsements for this book.

I also owe a debt of gratitude to the Chair of World Languages and Cultures department at Bronx Community College, Dr. Alexander Lamazares, for not only guiding me through the tenure and promotion process, but also for creating an enjoyable environment in which Faculty and staff can flourish and blossom.

In order to succeed in the academic world, professors need mentors who can congratulate them when they achieve great things, gently remind them when they mess up, constantly encourage them to be productive, and show them the way that leads to success. I would like to thank my incredible mentor Dr. Alicia Bralove Ramírez who propelled me to keep writing, to do better, and to go higher. Her crucial feedback on the draft of this book is very much appreciated.

I would like to thank my sisters and brothers as well as their spouses for their love and support throughout my academic career: Darline Guerrier-Carlin, Hamelie Elisabeth Guerrier-Desty and her husband Abed-Négo Desty, James Edler Guerrier and his wife Manise Clesca-Guerrier, Washner Guerrier and his wife Amir Blot, Vardalie Maharaï Guerrier, Gaspard Martholy Guerrier, and Marley Davidson Guerrier.

Introduction

Haiti is a geographically small, developing, and resilient country. The Haitian historian, playwright, novelist, songwriter, poet, and activist Jean-Claude Martineau (1937–) has often asserted that Haiti is the only country on earth that has a last name: "The poorest country in the Western Hemisphere."[1] However, the process by which Haiti became the recipient of so many misfortunes is not necessarily easily discernible. In order to really understand the development of Haiti's political, economic, and social structures, one would do well by focusing on five key events: the colonization of Saint-Domingue (1659–1804), the Haitian Revolution (1791–1804) and its aftermath, the United States Occupation (1915–1934), the Duvalier dictatorships, (1957–1986) and the rise of Jean-Bertrand Aristide (1953–) and democracy. This book examines critical historical issues through selected authors who present, analyze, project, defend, challenge and reject contrasting tropes about Haiti and Haitians in their works. It is in this context that I chose to examine works from six different writers: Massillon Coicou (1867–1908), Aimé Césaire (1913–2008), Jacques Roumain (1907–1944), Anne-Christine d'Adesky (1958–), Jean-Claude Martineau (1937–), and Emmanuel Védrine, (1959–). Taken together, these literary works will help comprehend some of the multiple topics that shaped Haitian thought and culture from 1892 to 1994. I use an eclectic approach by using terms borrowed from Postcolonialism, Poetics, Linguistics, and History. When analyzed from a postcolonial perspective, these works help to show the impact of colonization and slavery on Haitian thought, the interference of the international community in Haiti's affairs, the dictatorial aspects of the Duvalier regimes, and the efforts by Haitian citizens to improve their lives and reject hegemonic influences. This study will also point out facets of linguistic issues in Haiti with respect to the uses of Haitian Creole and French, and what some writers have done and continue to do in order to include as many Haitians as possible in the debates.

In spite of its opulence and beauty, Haitian literature remains, for the most part, unknown and under studied. It is written in French, Haitian Creole, English, Spanish, and Portuguese. This work will show the linguistic plurality of this literature and the tensions that arise from it. This study is significant because the translation of the works presented here written in French and Haitian Creole into English will provide the Anglophone world the opportunity to be exposed to distinguished Haitian writings that might otherwise be challenging to access. Unless otherwise indicated, all translations are made by the author. Each work selected proposes another dimension to the multiple issues that the Haitian people have faced and continue to face. All the authors studied in this book represent a form of resistance against illegitimate power or dictatorship. The time frame and historic events (as well as their aftermaths) were selected on the basis of their potential as quintessential, foundational cornerstones which taken together, will aid the reader toward developing a familiarity with the nexus of Haitian history and some of the literature that it produced. It is my hope that this work will make it possible for additional readings for readers who choose to pursue that avenue.

Divided into six chapters, this study focuses on some of the literary works published between 1892 and 1994[2] to show the diversity of Haitian and non-Haitian literature in different languages, periods, genres, and how many writers have used their works to identify problems, document certain events, challenge their compatriots to think critically about their situations, fight for their rights, and reflect on colonial legacy.

The first chapter, titled "Massillon Coicou: A Reflection on Slavery and Christianity," examines Massillon Coicou's poem *"Complaintes d'Esclave"* "The Slave's Lament," which is an introspection as well as a reflection on slavery, Blackness, God, and the Bible. In this poem the speaker, who is a Black slave, cries out to God and Death in vain to rescue him. Out of frustration, he questions God and God's mercy. Through an analysis of this poem, I show how one slave articulates his reaction to the colonizer's efforts to demonize him and perpetuate his bondage. This poem shines a light on the impact of colonization on Haitians as well as the role of Christian religion in their community.

As the second chapter will show, building a country after slavery was a formidable task. There were diverging opinions about how to proceed.

The second chapter, "The notion of Power in *The Tragedy of King Christophe* of Aimé Césaire" underlines Aimé Césaire's (1913–2008) manner of mixing the comic and the tragic, the serious and the burlesque as well his combined use of dance, song, gesture and speech. Although Aimé Césaire is a Martinican writer, his 1963 play, *The Tragedy of King Christophe* is used in this work because it offers an optic of the power struggle between Henri Christophe (1767–1820) and Alexandre Pétion (1770–1818), which is an interesting examination of the Haitian mentality in the early aftermath of the post revolution as perceived by others in the Caribbean. Césaire's work helps to make sense of the depth of political tensions in Haiti at that time. In this chapter, I highlight the tactics used by Henri Christophe to gain, exert and try desperately to hold on to his power, and show how Césaire understood as few can, the deleterious underpinnings of colonialism, and the struggles involved in forging a Haitian identity that defined itself on its own terms as it tried to heal from the traumas that it inherited as a nation.

If tensions among Haitian leaders prevented the country from reaching its full potential after the assassination of Emperor Jean-Jacques Dessalines, the American occupation of Haiti and the involvement of the Catholic Church in Haitian lives complicated the situation further and sparked a revolt among certain Haitian writers. The following chapter will highlight the rebellious works of Jacques Roumain against the American occupation as well as the Catholic Church.

In Chapter 3, "The Esthetics of Protest: Jacques Roumain's Literary Indictment of the American Occupation of Haiti and the Haitian Catholic Church," I use Roumain's poem *"Nouveau Sermon Nègre"* "New Negro Sermon" to illustrate his fight against one of the institutions he often criticized: the Church. I argue that throughout the poem Roumain draws parallels between the hardships of Blacks and the hardships of Christ. By doing so, he seeks to create a *New Negro Sermon* that challenges Black people to abandon the gospel of resignation in order to become active Christians in their communities. This chapter addresses the American occupation of Haiti and Roumain's reaction to it. An engaged poet, Roumain stood up against the American occupation and exposed the ruses of the occupiers as well as the crimes they committed. He also defended the Voodoo religion that was demonized by the Catholic Church. His work helped to shape the thought process of many of his contemporaries.

Twenty-three years after the American occupation of Haiti, the country was ruled by two dictators who oppressed Haitians for 29 years. The following chapter helps to understand the scope of the crimes committed by such regimes and focuses on a group of people often neglected in accounts of oppressed individuals under the Duvalier dynasty: women.

Chapter 4, "The Representation of Women's struggles during the Duvalier Regimes: Anne-Christine d'Adesky's Feminist Perspective in *Under the Bone*," studies Anne-Christine d'Adesky's (1958–X) *Under the Bone*, a book that she dedicates to Duvalier's many deceased victims in which the author explores post-Duvalier Haiti, by presenting characters whose mission consists of uncovering the truth about disappeared activists. Throughout the novel, she refers to numerous grave violations of human rights, illustrating the corruption and reign of terror that arose in Haitian society during both Duvalier regimes (1957–1986) as well as their immediate aftermath. I argue that by utilizing an eclectic narrative approach to demonstrate the plight of Haitian women, d'Adesky tackles the theme of imprisonment to unearth the atrocity and injustice Haitian women faced during the Duvalier dictatorships. Her fictionalized account includes stories, memos, letters, interior monologues, medical and legal documents, and taken together, they offer a plausible account of how Haitian women have actively contributed to the struggle against political oppression. D'Adesky's work transcends any single approach, applying autobiographical, philosophical, and psychoanalytic approaches. Her linguistic choice is significant, because English brings her work into the venue to publicize the injustices of Haiti for the English-speaking world. Her novel transcends linguistic, territorial, and critical approaches. In other words, it is part of cross-disciplinary conversations.

The Duvalier regimes caused many Haitians to flee the country in great numbers. In search of freedom and job opportunities, many Haitians went to the United States while others went to the Dominican Republic. In the next chapter, the analysis of Martineau's song helps us evaluate the impact of Haitian migration to the Dominican Republic on Haitian families.

In Chapter 5, "Jean-Claude Martineau: Songs as warnings," I analyze one of Jean-Claude Martineau's songs "*Vyewo*." I argue that while many writers tend to focus on the mistreatment of Haitians by the Dominican government and their harsh conditions in the bateyes,[3] Jean-Claude Martineau takes a different path. Instead, he insists on the heavy cross that wives have to bear in the absence of their husbands. In a subtle way, he shows the psychological impact of such a difficult situation on children, families, and relationships. By doing so, he adds another dimension to the debate about Haitian migration to the Dominican Republic. This chapter discusses the multiple causes of Haitian migration at that time. It also shows Jean-Claude Martineau's (1937–X) multiple efforts to valorize and promote Haitian Creole. Martineau proves that songs can be used as a medium to raise awareness.

Like Jean-Claude Martineau, Emmanuel Védrine believes that writing in Haitian Creole and using poetry can be an effective tool to educate the masses. That is what the next chapter will illustrate.

Chapter 6, "Time for Action: '*Manman, pa ban m tete ankò*'" (Mother, stop breastfeeding me), analyzes Emmanuel W Védrine's poem entitled "*Manman, pa banm tete ankò*" ("Mother, stop breastfeeding me"). It is a very short poem that depicts the complicated relationship between a mother and her child. The narrator expresses the feeling of a child who no longer sees breastfeeding as necessary. He demands real food from his mother in order to fully develop. From the start, he positions himself as the person who is in command. One quickly understands that he is no longer the passive, obedient child, but the revolutionary who is standing up for his rights. I argue that there are many ways to interpret this poem. It can be seen as a simple poem that talks about tensions between a child and his mother. Some people, however, might claim that the mother symbolizes anyone in a position of power: a boss, a partner, an NGO, a government, a colonial power etc. Since the subject matter is Haiti, the poem can be read as a national or international allegory if we interpret the child in the poem as Haiti and the mother as an NGO, the MINUSTAH,[4] a colonial power or an international force. In that sense, the poem suggests that Haiti doesn't need superficial help anymore. Because it has to stand on its feet and grow, it needs resources that can help it be strong against adversity. It needs economic and political independence in order to grow as a true nation. It cannot be treated like a child who keeps receiving baby food. It wants freedom to make its own decisions and develop as other nations do. Védrine's poem seems to indicate that if a child can stand up for his rights, everyone can do the same. Words have power and strong resistance can bring real changes.

Notes

[1] Maguire, Robert. "Toward the End of Poverty in Haiti." United States Institute of Peace. December 1, 2008. <https://www.usip.org/publications/2008/12/toward-end-poverty-haiti>

[2] The year 1892 was chosen as the starting point because it was the year that Coicou's poem was published, a work that helps us understand the suffering of slaves during colonization of Haiti and its impact on future Haitians. As for the ending date (1994), it is the year that d'Adesky's work was published, all the other works were published before 1994. D'Adesky's work helps us understand the negative impact of the Duvalier regimes on Haitians and the power that the Haitian army exerted on the Haitian population in the early 1990s.

[3] Working in a batey, a sugar cane field, is not an easy task: the sun is hot; the sugarcane leaves can cut the skin and cause bleeding, which can lead to infections if not properly treated. Any mistake made by the cane cutter with the machete can result in finger cuts or serious injuries. The workers know how dangerous such a job can be, but they sacrifice their lives in an attempt to provide for their families.

[4] The United Nations Stabilization Mission in Haiti, also known as MINUSTAH, an acronym of the French name, was a UN peacekeeping mission in Haiti that was in operation from 2004 to 2017.

Massillon Coicou: A Reflection on Slavery and Christianity

Introduction

This chapter will discuss the colonizing effects of language within the context of Haitian history. In discussing the role of language in his seminal work *Black Skin, White Masks*, Frantz Fanon (1925–1961), a renowned Martinican psychiatrist, philosopher and revolutionary analyzed the role of language and concluded that it is often a "vessel" which carries and reveals racism in culture. He posited that one cannot learn and speak a language without subconsciously accepting the cultural signs embedded in formulas of purity equaling whiteness and malevolence with Blackness.[1] (Fanon 1) Moreover, he believed that language possesses colonizing effects. In this chapter, I will show how these effects can be viewed in the poetry of Massillon Coicou.

Biography of Massillon Coicou

Jean Baptiste Massillon Coicou (1867–1908) was born on October 7, 1867, in Port-au-Prince. By all accounts, he grew up in a loving and intellectual family. He attended primary school at Les Frères de L'Instruction Chrétienne and secondary school at the Lycée Alexandre Pétion. Haitian students of his era were avid readers and are characterized by fervent patriotic sentiment. Since military service was required by the government, after completing his military service in 1891, Coicou was appointed professor at the Lycée Alexandre Pétion. In that school, he was the Chair of literature and social sciences. However, teaching did not prevent him from writing during his spare time. In fact, in 1892, Coicou published his collection of poems called *"Poésies nationales"* which was well-received by his contemporaries. Four years later (1896), his drama *"Les Fils de Toussaint"* was staged. In 1900, Coicou was named secretary and Chargé d'affaires of the

Haitian delegation to Paris. His dramatic poem called *"L'Oracle"* was published in 1901. In France, he continued to write literature and in 1903, he published two collections of poems called *"Passions"* and *"Impressions."* In 1904, he returned to Haiti and took the opportunity to found the newspaper *L'œuvre* and open the Library called "Amica" which bore his mother's name. Such an endeavor worried the Haitian government of Pierre Nord Alexis (1820–1910). While teaching Philosophy (1904–1908), Coicou made a serious effort to use theater[2] to educate the youth about their rights, their obligations, and the importance of patriotism. Among his most famous works as playwright figure *"Liberté"* and *"L'Alphabet"* (social drama 1905), *"L'Empereur Dessalines"* (historical drama 1907), *"Vincent de Paul"* (historical drama 1907), *"Féfé candidat et Féfé ministre"* and *"L'École mutuelle."*

According to the literary critics Eddy Arnold Jean and Justin O. Fièvre, "Massillon Coicou was a brilliant lecturer whose captivating words won him the esteem and admiration of Parisian intellectual circles."[3] (Jean and Fièvre, 47) They suggest that, by condemning foreign cultural influence and asking Haitians to be themselves, Coicou anticipated Dr. Jean Price Mars and can be seen as one of the precursors of the Indigenist movement. (Jean and Fièvre, 48)

Massillon Coicou was a Haitian poet, playwright, politician, and journalist, known for his keen sense of social justice, civic courage, and desire to defend and regenerate his country. It is in this context that Jean and Fièvre wrote:

> Massillon Coicou could not remain indifferent to the spectacle of the country governed by backward-looking tyrants. Loyal to the leader Firmin, and disgusted by the misdeeds of the Nord Alexis regime, he joined the opposition. He advocated the introduction of democracy for the benefit of the greatest number, presided over by an intellectual.[4] (p. 48)

His collection of poems entitled *Poésies nationales* (*National Poetry* 1892) concentrated on retelling Haitian history and the struggle for independence. In his poems, Coicou denounced civil war and promoted unity, peace, and progress. He was a powerful activist against colonialism and imperialism. The Haitian critic Ghislain Gouraige writes that Coicou's historical dramas on Haitian themes, his social satires, and poetry were often a "condemnation of his time, the poverty of the peasants, the exile of the better classes [to Europe] and the blind exercise of criminal power."[5] (quoted in Kennedy, 7) Coicou's search for the truth and his attempt to bring about progressive political changes in Haiti cost him his life. On March 15, 1908, Coicou was taken from his home in the middle of the night and brought to a cemetery to be executed along with his two brothers Horace and Louis: "This sincerely religious man, a professor of philosophy who put his convictions to work in such projects as teaching the illiterate of Port-au-Prince to read, paid dearly for being so outspoken." (Kennedy, 7) His Death did not go unnoticed by the Haitian population. As mentioned by Jean and Fièvre:

> The entire Republic mourned the Death of Massillon Coicou. His assassins ensured his immortality. In the History of Haiti, he remains the model of the haughty temperament, the implacable adversary of compromise, the symbol of the intransigent patriot, the irreducible enemy of tyrants.[6]

"*Complaintes d'Esclave*" ("The Slave's Lament")

Massillon Coicou was a poet who extensively reflected on the notion of freedom. He never missed an opportunity to talk about what his ancestors accomplished in order to end slavery. His collection entitled *Poésies nationales (Première série)* was dedicated to *l'Association du Centenaire de l'Indépendance Nationale*. Coicou wrote several poems about the liberation of slaves. For example, in *"Vertières,"* he highlights the plight of the slaves and praises the Haitian heroes who fought courageously to defeat the Napoleon Army. Likewise, in *"Le supplice du Noir"*, he describes a vivid scene in which a colonizer uses angry dogs to devour slaves and invites his friends to assist in this bloody act. I choose to analyze the poem *"Complaintes d'esclave"*, published in 1892, because it depicts some of the horrible crimes committed by the colonizers, the slave's thirst for freedom, and the slave's struggle with the Christian faith.

Although Coicou died young, he left behind a rich body of work that continues to fascinate literary critics and scholars. This essay will examine his poem *"Complaintes d'Esclave"* ("The Slave's Lament") which is an introspection as well as a reflection on slavery, Blackness, God, and the Bible. In this poem the speaker, who is a Black slave, cries out to God and Death in vain to rescue him. Out of frustration, he questions God and God's mercy. Through an analysis of this poem, I will show how one slave articulates his reaction to the colonizer's efforts to demonize him and perpetuate his bondage.

The poem is made of alexandrines (metrical lines composed of 12 syllables), a form used to express a serious topic, a dramatic tone. The title, which consists of two words "Complaintes d'esclave," gives the reader an idea of the theme that will be developed in the poem. The word *"complaintes,"* used in its plural form, indicates that many reproaches will be made in a repetitive manner. The term *"esclave"* refers to a person who is deprived of freedom and has to obey all of his master's commands. If not, a variety of punishments or even Death can follow. The poem, originally written in French, is divided into six parts: each one starts with a refrain that has four lines and is followed by a strophe of six lines. The refrain has the following rhyme scheme: ABAB. As for the strophes, they follow this rhyme pattern: CDDCEE. Since the refrain is repeated in all the six parts of the poem, I would like to start with it before analyzing each stanza separately. The repetition of the refrain in all the sections of the poem indicates that the speaker is still in search of an answer to the puzzling question:

> *Pourquoi donc suis-je nègre? Oh! pourquoi suis-je noir?*
> *Lorsque Dieu m'eut jeté dans le sein de ma mère,*
> *Pourquoi la mort jalouse et si prompte au devoir*
> *N'accourut-elle pas l'enlever de la terre?* (Coicou, 49)
>
> Why am I a Negro? Oh, why am I Black?
> When God cast me in my mother's womb
> Why did watchful Death not rush her to the tomb? (Kennedy, 8)

In the refrain, the word "*pourquoi*" is repeated three times and there are three question marks. Likewise, the words "*nègre*" and "*noir*" are mentioned in the first line in two questions. It is worth pointing out that "Noir" is a term used to refer to Black people in general. However, "Nègre" is often seen as a racial slur, a pejorative term in the context of slavery and colonialism. The speaker starts by questioning his color, God, and Death. He claims that God is responsible for his suffering by making him Black and argues: "*Mais Dieu m'a condamné, le sort doit me poursuivre*" (Coicou, 49) "But God condemned me, destiny pursues me." He also reproaches Death, who is usually seen as a liberator and savior, for not rescuing him. The speaker feels betrayed by both God and Death for their inactivity to change his destiny.

The term "Black" has negative connotations stemming from historically racist constructs via language to reinforce a racial hierarchy where "Black" would occupy a permanent place at the lowest end of the totem pole and white, the antithesis of Black, would reign supreme. But in this poem, the term "Black" is amplified because it is associated with subjugation and slavery. The speaker realizes that because of his Blackness, he becomes a living possession, an instrument of production. He wishes he had died in his mother's womb in order to avoid the inhuman conditions that slaves knew all too well. The self-hatred that he develops might be a reaction to the damage of being enslaved and oppressed. He dislikes his Blackness because society has made him associate his identity with the suffering that he has endured. Therefore, he equates escaping his identity with escaping from the pain and the suffering he has experienced. The fact that Coicou provided the slave with a direct voice was an unusually bold and innovative technique in 1898 and within Haitian literature in general.

All six parts of the poem provide the continuation of the speaker's lamentation.

Je n'aurais pas connu tous ces tourments affreux;
Mon cœur n'aurait pas bu tant de fiel, goutte à goutte.
Au fond de mon néant, oh! je serais, sans doute,
Moins plaintif, plus heureux.
Mais Dieu m'a condamné, le sort doit me poursuivre;
De mon sang, de mes pleurs, il faut que tout s'enivre! ... (Coicou, 49)

I would not have known this awful pain,
And drop by drop would not have drunk this gall,
This sense of utter nothingness...
But God condemned me, destiny pursues me,
Intoxicated by my blood, my tears! (Kennedy, 8–9)

In the first line of the strophe above, the past conditional (*Je n'aurais pas connu* ...) is used to express the regret of the narrator about his Blackness as well as his birth. Multiple nasal vowels are repeated in this strophe to stress the sense of lamentation. The vocabulary of despair and desperation is highlighted through words like: *tourments, affreux, fiel, néant, plaintif, condamné, poursuivre, pleurs*. Taken together, they show the horrible mental state of the narrator. He is in a constant state of misery because as a Black person he is tied to slavery and all the burdens that are associated with it. He feels cornered and does not see any way out. For this reason, he blames God who condemned him and caused him such a miserable life. The words "*sang*" and "*pleurs*" summarize the type of pressure he is under on a daily basis. His suffering is unbearable. The speaker compares his situation or status as a slave, someone's property, to that of bile. The way in which he refers to bodily fluid as a manifestation of a deeper pain is used several times throughout the poem. "And drop by drop (I) would not have drunk this gall." This is an allusion once again to a Death wish. He feels so diminished by his condition as a slave that he feels invisible. "This sense of utter nothingness..." that he feels is a direct result of the harshness of the systems of Western hegemony. He goes on to say, "Intoxicated by my blood, my tears!" The blood to which he refers symbolizes Death, but more so in the spiritual sense in that he is "intoxicated" with both blood and tears referring to the horrid, unbearable system of rendering another human being an object or property.

Where there is an emphasis placed on sorrow, burden, and hardship in the first stanza, the second one concerns representations of freedom as evidenced by images of birds, the wind, and water:

Car libre l'oiseau vole et redit ses concerts;
Car libre le vent souffle au gré de son caprice;

CHAPTER 1

> *Car libre, l'onde limpide, harmonieuse, glisse*
> *Entre les gazons verts.*
> *Esclave, il n'est pour moi nul bonheur, nulle fête,*
> *Et je n'ai pas de place où reposer ma tête.* (Coicou, 50)

> The bird is free to soar and freely sings,
> The wind is free to blow where e'er it will,
> The limpid waters, too, can flow through fields of green.
> Such happiness, such joy are not for me:
> I am a slave
> With nowhere to find rest excerpt the grave. (Kennedy, 9)

While contemplating nature, the narrator realizes that birds are free to spread their wings and fly as they please. The wind can blow wherever it wants. Likewise, water can flow as it wishes. The freedom of these natural elements is punctuated by the anaphora in the first three lines: "*Car libre....*" Verbs like "*vole,*" "*souffle,*" and "*glisse*" express the sense of freedom. Expressions such as *concerts, au gré de, caprice, limpide, harmonieuse, gazons verts* underline a calm environment in which everything is in order. However, reflecting on his life, the speaker only sees negativity. Happiness and celebrations are out of reach in his world. He can't even find a resting place. In the line "*Car libre l'oiseau vole et redit ses concerts*;" (Coicou, 50) the repetition of the explosive sound "r" translates the narrator's anger while contemplating nature. The alliteration or repetition of the soft sound "l" creates a calm atmosphere tied to a dream that he cannot enjoy. The "e" sound lengthens the sentence and exacerbates his restlessness. Such observation amplifies his sadness. The subject in this poem is made more aware of his own bondage by observing nature and the free agents within it (i.e., birds, wind, and water). He emphasizes the magnitude of his situation by concluding "I am a slave with nowhere to find rest except the grave."[7] The freedom that is accorded to the natural elements remains out of reach.

The third stanza names the narrator's oppressor "le colon" and underlines his cruelty:

> *Quand la voix du colon prend son lugubre accent,*
> *Quand siffle sur mon front sa flexible rouchine,*[8]
> *Si j'ose tressaillir en lui tendant l'échine,*
> *Il me bat jusqu'au sang.*
> *Et si, quand le fouet plonge en ma chair qu'il déchire,*
> *J'invoque sa pitié: J'entends le maître rire! ...* (Coicou, 50)

> When the master's voice takes on its mournful accent,
> When his flexible whip whistles on my forehead,
> If I dare to flinch and stretch my back,
> He beats me to a pulp.

> And if, when the whip plunges into my flesh it tears,
> I beg for mercy: I hear the master laugh! ... (My translation)

The adverb of time "*quand*" is repeated three times to indicate different moments during which the master acts against the slave. The repetition (three times) of the nasal vowels "an, en" in the line "*Quand la voix du colon prend son lugubre accent*" (Coicou, 50) indicates the master's anger toward the narrator. Likewise, the repetition (three times) of the hard sound "f" in the line "*Quand siffle sur mon front sa flexible rouchine*" expresses a harsh physical sound terrifying the narrator. In the following line "*Et si, quand le fouet plonge en ma chair qu'il déchire*" (Coicou, 50), the repetition of the high-pitched sound "i" emphasizes the scream, the squeak of the narrator. This suggests that any attempt at a reprisal by the narrator leads to a beating till he bleeds. The master is described as a pitiless individual who shows no sign of compassion when his whip is tearing off his slave's flesh. The expression "*J'entends le maître rire! ...*" suggests that the master takes pleasure in his slave's pain. The speaker provides a moving observation of his situation and the depth of his master's cruelty. Coicou employs personification by giving the master's "whip" "*le fouet*" humanlike qualities: "The whip sings till I bleed." In this situation the "singing" refers to the sound of "whipping" as well as the act of "whipping" the slave into submission. The juxtaposition between the previously mentioned freedom (that of birds, wind and water) and bondage is quite jarring and shows the reader just how distant/opposite these two poles are for this slave. His dream of freedom has suddenly ended because he is a slave "But no, God made me Black." What is particularly disturbing in the third stanza is the fact that the master takes pleasure in the slave's pain: "When I cry for mercy, it's not laughter that I need." This shows the master as a heartless human being ignoring any notion of empathy and justice. In discussing the condition of slaves, Jean and Fièvre mention that:

> Sometimes the settler beats him out of a spirit of barbarism, out of simple sadistic satisfaction. A whole arsenal of coercive measures, a whole apparatus of repression is put in place to force docility. Cruelties were multiplied: rods, flames, irons, shootings, drownings, hangings. The slightest peccadillo was a hanging case, depending on the colonist's mood.[9] (p. 52)

The fourth strophe has a different tone. It is a reference to a dream that the narrator had in which he was free.

> *Cette nuit, cependant, j'ai vu la liberté! ...*
> *L'esclave ne dort pas; mais un labeur sans trêve*
> *M'ayant brisé les sens, j'ai joui de ce rêve*

CHAPTER 1

> *Que l'on m'a tant vanté:*
> *J'étais libre, j'errais, comme le maître, allègre,*
> *Ayant l'espace, à moi! Mais non, Dieu m'a fait nègre ...* (Coicou, 51)

> Last night I dreamt of Liberty,
> Of freedom from this endless toil.
> Joyously I roamed, no longer slave,
> Through spaces, places that were mine!
> But no, God made me Black. (Kennedy, 9)

The expression "*la liberté*" ends with an exclamation point to express his strong emotion of joy in that dream. The expression "*Que l'on m'a tant vanté*" suggests that the speaker heard about freedom and how wonderful such a feeling is. In that dream, like the master, he was free and had his own space. However, very quickly reality sets in. Since God made him a Black person, his fate is tied to endless labor, beatings, and contempt. Such harsh reality causes his sorrow.

In the midst of his misery, the narrator turns to God and His teaching to find rest:

> *Où donc es-tu, toi-même? On m'a dit que, d'en bas,*
> *Lorsqu'une âme qui prie est souffrante et sincère,*
> *Vers toi qu'on nomme, ô Dieu! peut monter sa prière:*
> *Et tu ne m'entends pas! ...*
> *La prière du nègre a-t-elle moins de charmes?*
> *Ou n'est-ce pas à toi que s'adressent ses larmes?* (Coicou, 51)

> Where are you, Lord? When a soul that prays
> From here below is suffering and true,
> I'm told his prayers rise straight to You.
> But you do not hear!
> Have Negro prayers no weight against this awful fate? (Kennedy, 10)

In this strophe, the speaker addresses God directly using the following terms: "*tu*," "*toi-même*," "*ô Dieu*." Using three questions, he reproaches God's absence in the suffering of Black people. The expression "*On m'a dit que*" is a reference to believers who claim that God hears prayers and comes to the rescue of his servants. He uses biblical language to reiterate that something seems to be wrong because "*Lorsqu'une âme qui prie est souffrante et sincère*" (Coicou, 51), God is supposed to hear his cry and answer his prayer. Out of frustration, he decries "*Et tu ne m'entends pas! ... .*" The last two lines question God's attitude toward Black people, asking if Black people's prayer is less relevant to God. He feels that Black people's tears don't seem to affect God much. So, he is under the impression that

God does not intervene to rescue Black people from their horrible condition. That is a great disappointment for him.

Since there is no form of solace for the slave on earth, he turns to what he perceives as hope, which he believes takes place in a spiritual realm. In fact, a spiritual thread runs through the poem as well and is made more evident in the last two stanzas where the slave begins to question God and His mercy. It is clear that the slave is testing God and His word by making a direct reference to Psalm 36 verse 6 that states: "This poor man cried out, and the Lord heard him, and saved him out of all his troubles." This biblical verse also brings to mind the passage in Exodus in which the cries of the people of Israel reached God's ears. The speaker has heard of God's ability to hear the poor man's cries and His capacity to perform miracles. However, because of God's lack of response to his multiple requests, out of frustration, he starts to question whether God hears when a Black slave cries out to Him. It is common knowledge that Christianity was used not only to justify but also to reinforce the institution of slavery. "Slaves, obey your earthly masters with fear and trembling" (Ephesians 6:5), or "tell slaves to be submissive to their masters and to give satisfaction in every respect" (Titus 2:9) are just two examples of how the Bible was appropriated by Europeans with the goal of promulgating the domination of other groups of people such as enslaved Africans and others. Many slaves and even many oppressed people who are Christians still believe that their difficult lives due in part to injustice (more specifically racism), will be rewarded after Death with entrance into heaven. Coicou touches on this stating:

> *Ah! si tu m'entends bien, tu dois aussi me voir.*
> *Si je blasphème, hélas! tu vois bien que je pleure?*
> *Tu sais, toi qui sais tout, que je souffre à toute heure,*
> *Parce que je suis noir!*
> *Eh bien, oui, trop longtemps j'ai souffert sans mot dire.*
> *Seigneur, pardonne-moi si j'apprends à maudire.* (Coicou, 52)

> If You hear me You can see me, too.
> If I curse, alas! You see that I am weeping.
> All-Knowing, You must know my endless pain!
> My silent suffering, Lord, has been so long and great
> You must forgive me, if I've learned to hate! (Kennedy 10)

In this strophe, the narrator refers to the three great qualities of God: his omniscience *"tu sais tout,"* his omnipotence *"pardonne-moi"* (his ability to pardon), and his omnipresence *"tu me vois," "tu m'entends."* His argument is that since God is everywhere, knows everything, and can do everything, he knows well about his misery, and suffering. The mention of the present tense *"je pleure," "Je souffre"* and the past tense *"J'ai souffert"* underline a suffering that started in the past and continues in the present. The expression *"trop longtemps"* highlights an indefinite period of time spent under such dire conditions and the color of his skin is the cause of his misery: *"Parce que je suis noir!"* In the midst of his frustration, knowing that he casts doubt on God regarding his mercy, he asks him for forgiveness for his insolence. The slave is concerned about his salvation in the midst of being subjected to hell on earth. Hate begets hate; it is quite simple, and it is rather challenging to apply the "turn the other cheek" mentality when faced with such inhumane cruelty by those in power. He doubts that God hears his prayer and sees what he is enduring. Nevertheless, he asks for forgiveness because his hatred might prevent him from reaching heaven.

Conclusion

This poem is a long monologue in which the narrator reflects on his life as a slave. His introspective thought is deep and gives the reader insight into his suffering. In this poem, the slave externalizes his sufferings by articulating his pain and misery. He raises the question in his anguished cry: "Why do I suffer? Why must I suffer because of the color of my skin?" Racial awareness is therefore made explicit. The speaker does not deny the existence of God but simply reproaches God for not easing his troubles. In doing so, he expresses the feeling of many slaves who prayed to God for years asking for freedom and left with their prayers unanswered. Furthermore, the slave's cry seems to be that of the entire Black race who were humiliated throughout the world and treated as inferior. The poet suggests that Christianity was used to justify and to reinforce the institution of slavery. Through this work, Massillon Coicou also challenges Matthew 7 verse 7, which states: "Ask and it will be given to you; seek and you will find; knock and the door will be opened to you." It is accurate to state that Coicou's poem acts as a condemnation of how unendurable life was for slaves. Nevertheless, the slave in this poem asks for forgiveness, which shows the extent to which he internalized the mistreatment and exploitation to which he was subjected to such a great degree that his fear of reprisal permeated the poem. Massillon Coicou's poem provides two possible solutions to the slave's unbearable and unrelenting suffering. One is by reversing life or dying. One could argue that the torture of this life was so egregious that Death would actually provide some form of relief. The other option is to completely embrace spiritual teachings that were forced upon slaves. If life can be seen as a state in between Death and a possible spiritual afterlife, the common denominator in all realms is language, which is heavily laden with colonial constructs and binary judgments.

Notes

1. Fanon notes that, "Doesn't white symbolize justice, truth, and virginity? ... The white man practices this logic daily. The Black man is the symbol of evil and ugliness." (page 157)

    Fanon, Frantz. *Black Skin, White Masks*. Translated from the French by Richard Philcox. Grove Press, 2008.

2. Theresa V. Jeffress wrote that: "The Theater may be considered as the 'genre par excellence' of 'le culte de la patrie'. Massillon Coicou, ardent nationalist, founder of 'le théâtre Haïtien' and 'La Bibliothèque Amica', one of Haiti's two national Libraries, may be logically selected as the most outstanding of Haitian writers in the realm of theater." (p. 3)

    Jeffress, Theresa V. *Massillon Coicou, the Writer and Patriot*. Master's Thesis. Columbia University, 1945.

3. Jean and Fièvre: "Massillon Coicou fut un brillant conférencier dont le verbe captivant a conquis l'estime, l'admiration des milieux intellectuels parisiens."

    Jean, Eddy Arnold and Fièvre, Justin O. *Histoire de la littérature haïtienne. Le mouvement patriotique*. Tome II. Editions Terre Neuve, 1986.

4. Jean and Fièvre: "Massillon Coicou ne pouvait rester indifférent au spectacle de la Patrie gouvernée par des tyrans rétrogrades. Fidèle au leader Firmin, et écœuré par les méfaits du régime de Nord Alexis, il rallia l'opposition. Il préconisa l'instauration de la démocratie au profit du plus grand nombre, présidée par un intellectuel."

    Jean, Eddy Arnold and Fièvre, Justin O. *Histoire de la littérature haïtienne. Le mouvement patriotique*. Tome II. Editions Terre Neuve, 1986.

5. Kennedy, Ellen Conroy. *The Negritude Poets: An Anthology of Translations from the French*. New York: Thunder's mouth Press, 1989.

6. "La République entière pleura la mort de Massillon Coicou. Ses assassins lui ont assuré l'immortalité. Il demeure dans L'Histoire d'Haïti le modèle du tempérament altier, adversaire implacable de compromission, le symbole du patriote intransigeant, ennemi irréductible des tyrans." (p. 48)

    Jean, Eddy Arnold and Fièvre, Justin O. *Histoire de la littérature haïtienne. Le mouvement patriotique*. Tome II. Editions Terre Neuve, 1986.

7. "Esclave, il n'est pour moi nul bonheur, nulle fête, / Et je n'ai pas de place où reposer ma tête" (Coicou, 50)

8. According to Jacquelin Doclé, "Rouchine" is "creolism that translates the French words verge and fouet. Massillon Coicou chose it expressly to rhyme with échine." "*créolisme qui traduit les mots français verge et fouet. Massillon Coicou l'a choisi expressément pour rimer avec échine.*"

    (Dolcé, 28) Dolcé, Jacquelin. *Massillon Coicou: Textes choisis*. Editions Choucoune, 2000.

9. Jean and Fièvre: "Parfois le colon le bat par esprit de barbarie, par simple satisfaction de sadisme. Tout un arsenal de mesures coercitives, tout un appareil de répression est mis en place pour le contraindre à la docilité. On multiplie les cruautés: verges, flammes, fers, fusillades, noyages, pendaisons. La moindre peccadille équivalait à un cas pendable selon l'humeur du colon."

    Jean, Eddy Arnold and Fièvre, Justin O. *Histoire de la littérature haïtienne. Le mouvement patriotique*. Tome II. Editions Terre Neuve, 1986.

Bibliography

Coicou, Massillon. *Poésies nationales*. Imprimerie V. Goupy et Jourdain: Paris, 1892.

Dolcé, Jacquelin. *Massillon Coicou: Textes choisis*. Editions Choucoune, 2000.

Fanon, Frantz. *Black Skin, White Masks*. Translated from the French by Richard Philcox. Grove Press, 2008.

Jean, Eddy Arnold and Fièvre, Justin O. *Histoire de la littérature haïtienne. Le mouvement patriotique*. Tome II. Editions Terre Neuve, 1986.

Jeffress, Theresa V. *Massillon Coicou, the Writer and Patriot*. Master's Thesis. Columbia University, 1945.

Kennedy, Ellen Conroy. *The Negritude Poets: An Anthology of Translations from the French*. The Vikings Press, 1975.

CHAPTER 2

The Notion of Power in *The Tragedy of King Christophe* of Aimé Césaire

Introduction

Aimé Césaire's poetry, plays and critical essays are widely discussed in academia, and continue to reverberate among readers throughout the worldwide French reading and theater going public. His lengthy life (1913–2008) bore witness to many historical events in the Caribbean, and his writing is characterized by an original optic that often presents multiple perspectives on a single issue or event. These perspectives are often at odds among themselves,[1] but taken together present an oddly cohesive narrative. His play *The Tragedy of King Christophe*, written in 1963, is a work that although fictional, nonetheless provides insight into certain aspects of a collective Haitian history after the revolution. Léon-François Hoffmann states, "It was in Santo Domingo that the only successful slave revolt in human history took place, and in 1804 the first independent country in the New World after the United States was founded." (Hoffmann, 9) However, after the assassination of Jean-Jacques Dessalines (1758–1806), the first head of the Haitian state in 1806, the country found itself in an onerous situation. There was a widespread and pervasive debate about who should replace Dessalines, and after disputes between the rivals Henri Christophe (1767–1820) and Alexandre Pétion (1770–1818), the country was divided into two parts. Christophe abandoned the southern half of the country to his rival Alexandre Pétion. He was President of Haiti (1806–1811), then King of Haiti (1811–1820). Pétion became president in the south (1806–1818). The two political leaders in the play represent the two schools of thought on how to handle life after slavery. The concept of the perpetuation of a monarchy can easily be traced to colonial ties, and it is in this context that Césaire's play is set. The purpose of this chapter is to examine the notion of power in Césaire's play.

CHAPTER 2

Biography of Aimé Césaire

The scholar Romuald Fonkoua is widely known to have written the most comprehensive biography about Aimé Césaire.[2] His book provides great details about Césaire's relatives, friends, his studies, and his connections in France and in the Antilles as well as analysis of some of his works. Born in Basse-Pointe, Martinique, Aimé Fernand David Césaire was one of the most beloved Martinican writers. Poet, playwright, politician, and teacher he had a great impact on Martinican politics and culture. At an early age, he had a significant social and financial advantage compared to other students of his time. However, this advantage was not a factor in his specific educational formation as he attended a school with other students of greater prosperity. As suggested by Conroy Kennedy: "Césaire's family was of a slightly more prosperous class. His father was a minor government clerk, his mother a dressmaker. From an early age, their son attended on a scholarship, a school frequented by the children of far richer families." (Kennedy, 62) In 1931, after receiving a thorough and rigorous education in Martinique at the Lycée Schoelcher, "At 18, already known as a brilliant student, he went on a scholarship to France. After studying at the Lycée Louis-le-Grand, he went to the prestigious *École Normale Supérieure*, where he earned a *licence ès lettres*." (Kennedy, 62) His brilliance provided him with opportunities to network with people who shaped his visions and thought process, particularly in the realms of African history and culture and what they represent for Black identity. For example, "Senghor introduced Césaire to the modern European writers-Proust, James Joyce, Virginia Woolf-the surrealist poets, the American Negro Renaissance." (Kennedy, 62–63)

The youthful and energetic Césaire participated actively in many initiatives. In fact, in 1934, with his colleagues Léon Gontran Damas and Léopold Cédar Senghor, he created the literary review *L'Étudiant Noir* (The Black Student) in order to have a written forum about Negro awareness, their history, their traditions, their sufferings, and their needs: "In its March 1935 issue, Césaire published a passionate tract against assimilation in which he first coined the term 'Negritude.'"[3] (Quoted in *A Tempest*, VII). By 1935, he passed the entrance exam for the *École Normale Supérieure*. In 1939, he published his poem called "Cahier d'un retour au pays natal" in the Parisian periodical called *Volontés*. That publication was a complete success. The same year (1939), he moved back to his native land and started teaching in a High School at the capital. Teaching did not prevent him from writing. In fact, in 1941, with his wife Suzanne Roussi, he founded the literary review *Tropiques* in an attempt to promote Martinican identity. Fascinated by Césaire's work, the writer André Breton decided to promote it after having spent time on that Caribbean island. Teaching and writing were not the only matters that were on Césaire's mind. Politics was also an avenue he was eying: "Césaire's involvement in politics developed out of a seven-month visit to Haiti in 1944. Through the key figures of Toussaint L'Ouverture and Henri Christophe, and in spite of their tragic fates, Haiti symbolized for Césaire the possibility of a Caribbean political independence and cultural autonomy. While there, he lectured on Mallarmé and Rimbaud and absorbed what would eventually result in two works dealing with Haiti's history: The book-length essay *Toussaint Louverture: la révolution française et le problème social*, and his plays *La Tragédie du roi Christophe*." (Clayton Eshleman and Annette Smith, quoted in *Aimé Césaire. The Collected Poetry*, 3–4) Upon his return to Martinique, some of his friends invited him to give multiple lectures about Haiti. After doing so, in 1945, with the support of the French Communist Party (PCF), Césaire was elected mayor of Fort-de-France and deputy to the French National Assembly for Martinique. The critic Robin D. G. Kelley discusses in the introduction of *A Tempest*, x–xi how in 1946 Césaire experienced a significant setback in his political and social emergence. The victory of playing a fundamental role in overseeing the change in status of Guadeloupe, Guiana, and Réunion to Departments instead of colonies within the French Republic was short-lived. The reverse of what he had envisioned indeed took place-instead of fewer French officials in the colonies, they flocked there in greater numbers.[4] In 1947, he published his long and famous poem called "*Cahier d'un retour au pays natal*." Impressed by such work, André Breton wrote an introduction in which he praised the Martinican poet. In 1950, Césaire wrote *Discours sur le colonialisme* (Discourse on Colonialism) which is a denunciation of European colonial racism and hypocrisy. Césaire published multiple collections of poems such as: *Les Armes miraculeuses* (Miraculous Weapons), 1946; *Soleil Cou Coupé* (Beheaded Sun), 1948; *Ferrements* (Shackles), 1959; *Cadastre* (Land Survey), 1961. Likewise, as playwright, he also wrote several pieces of drama such as *La Tragédie du Roi Christophe* (The Tragedy of King Christophe), 1963, *Une Saison au Congo* (A Season in the Congo), 1966. For five years (1983–1988), he presided over the Regional Council of Martinique. His political career ended in 2001. In 2008, he died of a heart attack in Martinique. His funeral was a phenomenon. He was given the honor of a state funeral and thousands of people attended on April 20, 2008. Prior to his Death, in 2007, he witnessed the renaming of Martinique's airport to bear his name. Scholars such as Alioune Diop, Abiola Irele, and Lilyan Kesteloot stress that Césaire's work has had a tremendous impact on Blacks living in the Caribbean, in Europe, in the United States, as well as Africa.

CHAPTER 2

Exerting power

Césaire's play opens with an intriguing prologue that narrates an interactive cockfight with many spectators and commentators. The action is depicted in a *gagaire*, a place where cockfights take place. The animals involved in this fight are named after Christophe and Pétion. A *gagaire* is typically a place in which a raw mix of violence, aggression and joy are all manifest. When spectators who bet on a particular cock see that their choice is landing strong thrusts to its opponent, they usually rejoice. In Césaire's rendition, the spectators of this fight vociferously cheer either for Christophe or for Pétion. This cockfight highlights the struggle between Christophe and Pétion for power, and one purpose of Césaire's play is to highlight the tactics used by Henri Christophe to gain power and exert his dominance. In a *gagaire*, the cocks fight continuously until one overpowers the other. The cock that can administer the biggest blow to its opponent dominates the arena and wins the fight. Césaire's choice of a primitive metaphor is to be noted.

At the beginning of the first act, one notices, in fact, that the question of control is already addressed. Christophe describes his mulatto rival Pétion as a weakling who gives in to the demands of the ever-present French. The problem is that the animosity between these two men has negative repercussions for the entire country. At a moment in which unity was more important than ever, political strife and dissent presented formidable obstacles toward reaching and implementing a sustainable new social order. After long arguments, they separate, and each goes his own way. The underlying issue that affects all else in their collisions is that Christophe and Pétion are different in the way they handle power, and their vision for exercising it. For example, Christophe was looking for an independent state that did not have to answer to France. As for Pétion: "They say that to get the French King to recognize him, he's offered to pay reparations to the former colonists!" (I; 2, p. 14). There were other points of contrast between them as well. For example, Christophe differed from Pétion in his leadership. During the Civil War (1806), the opposition leader told Pétion: "Mr. President, it falls to your lot to persuade us: the assembly has the right to know, it is your duty to tell us all" (I; 6, p. 29). Pétion answers him: "I am a democrat, and I wish to be not the commander but rather the guide of our free nation. Therefore, the nation shall know all my thoughts; it is the nation that will decide, and when the nation has decided, I assure you, Pétion will take action!" (I, 6, p. 29). Christophe is therefore not as democratic as Pétion. He is a man who likes to give orders, and his philosophy is to rule alone to achieve his goals.

Although it is readily seen between Christophe and Pétion, the notion of power is present across all social strata in this play. In essence, there are two camps in this play. The first group is the government. These are the people who govern and only care about their own interests. In the second camp is the majority of the population, who are not in power and are subordinate to the first group.

Christophe is the representative of supremacy par excellence in this play. He uses three clearly identifiable strategies to gain and exercise clout. The first strategy is to have himself proclaimed king. Having understood the mechanics of the mulatto Senate in the west to control his authority as president, he moves north and is crowned king. This title allowed him to eliminate legislative restrictions. As the critic Marc-A. Christophe points out: "Holder of absolute power, he will, without passing through the lengthy process of parliamentary voting, enact a series of laws and decrees whose ultimate goal will be the prosperity of the land and the creation of a free, self-sufficient nation."[5] (Marc-A Christophe 32) Once crowned king, he demanded reverence from everyone. For example, on his birthday, while the bishop was congratulating him on his new home, Christophe interrupted him and said: "Yeah, yeah-old frock-hanger, when you talk to the Lord, you do it in Latin!" (I; 7, p.34)[6] So the bishop answers him in Latin. Césaire's ironic depiction of the insolent king displays his arrogance thus: "If I am King, it's not by the grace of God or the will of the people, but by the will and grace of my fists." (III; 3, p.81) His folly of grandeur is also shown when he meets the French messenger: "When you address yourself to me, Mr. Franco de Médina, you call me 'Sir.' You say, 'Your Majesty.'" (II; 5, p. 56)

The second strategy used by Christophe to show his power and scope was the construction of the citadel.[7] At the time, France was planning to invade Haiti to take back its former colony. Césaire depicts Christophe as aware that a united front together with Pétion may be the only way to obstruct France's objective. It is in that sense that Christophe says about Pétion: "I hope he will recognize that the moment has come to end our quarrel in order to build the country and unite this people against a danger, nearer than we had supposed, that could threaten its very existence." (I, 6, p. 28) Faced with such drastic news, Christophe decided to fight to the end to safeguard Haiti's independence. He wanted to show the greatness of his people by educating them and building a large citadel in Milot (a city located in the north of Haiti). This fort would serve as a military base to thwart the French armed forces in case of invasion. It would also be a symbol of resistance, hope and national pride. But, to realize this great project, Christophe used rigid, questionable and highly abusive means. For example, Césaire represents him as ordering that "everyone to work, to serve, to transport the stones. Ten stones a day for the women, that wouldn't kill them, no? Two to five per child, according to age." (II; 3, p. 51) We see here that he becomes more and more malicious and strict. In one instance, the foreman tells him that he has put a hundred men to hoist the pieces, but they can't. By way of reply, the king tells him:

"Take out 50 from the ranks: that will help." (II; 8, p.65) In commenting on the historical impact of King Christophe's policy on his people, Marc-A. Christophe writes "The new order the monarch wants to install is incompatible with civil liberties and individual freedom."⁸ (36) The construction of the citadel transforms Christophe little by little into a despot. This man of order and discipline does not hesitate to use force to obtain compliance to his orders.

The third strategy used by Césaire in the characterization of Christophe to exercise his power is through the manipulation of religion. He meddles in the private lives of his subjects and uses his power to force them to practice his doctrine. He is a Catholic and wants his workers to follow his definition of Catholic principles. In expressing concern about peasants having children without being married, he declares: "I don't want my subjects fooling around like that with their trousers down, like villagers! So, I have decided to marry you all at once." (II; 4, p. 54) Marriage then becomes mandatory and moreover, individuals must choose their partners on the spot. Marc-A. Christophe observes that:

> Thus, in Aimé Césaire's play we see a frantic attempt by Christophe to intervene in every aspect of the lives of his subjects. He decides what must be drunk in official ceremonies, the form of artistic creation, procreation in the kingdom and, in view of boosting agricultural production, he reattached the peasants to the land and created a special unit, the Royal Dahomey, to control their movements and to police the land.⁹ (p. 38)

In addition to the aforementioned schemes to hold on to his rule, Césaire's Christophe, who is so eager to rule others, does not follow the divine rules. He imprisoned Brelle, the priest, which resulted in his Death by starvation. This crime committed by Christophe did not go unpunished. The lightning thrown against the powder magazine, which caused Death and destruction, was one of God's responses to the king's wickedness. The latter becomes so angry that he raises his sword against the sky. As the Césaire scholar Alain Moreau indicates:

> In Apostrophizing Saint Peter, the bearer of the keys, the one who opens the doors of paradise, it is not only the God of the Christians that he assaults, it is not only the God of the Christians that he attacks, it is also as Marianne Bailey has shown, the gods of his country, the loa Legba, the one who makes the passage between the natural and the supernatural, the master of the conjurations at the crossroads.¹⁰ (Moreau, 286)

Christophe is a figure both majestic and monstrous. On the one hand, he wants to safeguard his independence and show the greatness and value of his fellow citizens. The critic Marc-A. Christophe questioned "How does one rebuild human nature? How does one overcome the negative inheritance of 300 years of slavery? A new order had to be created, a new mentality had to be invented, one that would transcend years of subservience and engender a new man."¹¹ (p. 33) King Christophe wanted to be that agent of change. Yet he is also monstrous because the means he uses to achieve his goal are inhuman. Marc-A Christophe said "From the outset, I would like to say that these measures are incompatible with human rights and civil liberties. But to be fully evaluated, they have to be understood in light of the psychological impact of 300 years of slavery on the new nation." (32) Christophe's ambition for power linked to his insolence leads his people and even the gods to abandon him. With this play, Césaire exposes the dysfunction of authoritarian power. Christophe ignores the most important problem of his people (i.e., survival) who ask for nothing more than a piece of land to cultivate. Obsessed with the desire to extend his power, he decides to rule alone. The Césaire scholar Moreau writes: "The character of Christophe is extremely complex. There is in him some Prometheus, some Peter the Great, some Bourgeois Gentilhomme." (281) Christophe wanted to bring drastic change to his new nation. However, he went about it too quickly because the people were not ready to switch mentality at such speed. Even the notion of freedom for them was different than what Christophe had thought. As Marc-A. Christophe rightly understands: "Unfortunately, freedom to the then uneducated and apolitical former slaves meant the right to rest and sleep the days away, the right not to work." (33) Christophe did not seem to understand that the new nation needed more time "to grow, to mature and bear its fruits." (Marc-A. Christophe 39) Instead of giving them time to breathe, to rest, and to adjust to a new system, he imposed hard labor during the construction of the citadel.

Conclusion

Césaire's work is complex when it comes to what politicians or those in power present as the problems of the Haitian people. These social issues are not, in fact, necessarily what the Haitian people themselves see as their problems. The Haitian people of the new nation saw common ground between all groups. This meant the desire to preserve freedom, independence, and to have a livelihood. Anecdotal evidence widely suggests that this was the desire of the vast majority of Haitians, regardless of race or profession. Even Christophe and Pétion agree on this point during their only meeting in the play. Had Christophe and Pétion considered themselves Haitians first, and had they put the interests of the nation first, Césaire might not have written a tragedy years later. Although Christophe had high hopes and aspirations for his people of Haiti, he did not employ even remotely human tactics to achieve his ideals. Haiti was supposed to be a safe paradise, a beacon of hope for all the slaves of the world because of the abolishment of slavery. Instead, the country ended up in turmoil. Christophe desperately tried to recreate the European courts in Haiti: "The creation of a nobility was supposed to establish the prestige of the kingdom, it only creates a class of parasites."[12] (Hervé Fuyet, 1108) According to the scholar Rodney E. Harris "For Césaire the important question of the twentieth century is that of decolonization and what comes after it."[13] (364) This play underlines the difficulty of building a nation after slavery and shows the effect of colonization and alienation on the new nation.

However, there are many aspects of Henri Christophe's life that Aimé Césaire's play did not depict. Césaire portrays Christophe as avaricious; However, the Historian Jean Fils-Aimé argues that contrary to many Haitian politicians, Henri Christophe did not use state funds to enrich himself or his family, but to serve his community.[14] In fact, continues Fils-Aimé, before becoming head of state, Christophe owned a maritime fleet of several dozen ships. When he became head of state, he donated ten boats to the Haitian state.[15] Fils-Aimé praises Christophe's placement of competent people at his side. This, in turn, contributed to a great sense of public management. Aimé Césaire seems to make fun of King Christophe for establishing a kingdom in Haiti and following a European model of government. However, what Césaire fails to acknowledge, as the scholar Yven Destin acknowledges, "Christophe believed that if a kingdom such as Britain could do more to abolish slavery than France and the United States, Haitians might be better off within a kingdom."[16] (193) It is worth pointing out that some of the great accomplishments of King Christophe do not figure in Césaire's work. For example, under the reign of Christophe, Haiti was a refuge for Black people coming from the United States:

> In light of an abolition movement rising in the United States, Prince Saunders helped connect Christophe to organizations that advanced the relocation of Black US freedmen to Haiti. Long before Haitian president Boyer did so, Christophe was the first leader to open Haiti to enslaved Blacks and freedmen, offering them asylum on Haitian soil.[17] (Destin 194)

In his play, Césaire undermines the diplomatic relations Christophe had with certain world leaders as well as the economic prosperity under the Kingdom of Christophe. According to scholar Yven Destin, Christophe established "amicable relations with the British and the Germans. He also created a trading partnership between Haiti and Jamaica, constructed the Citadelle fortress and Sans Souci palace, and recruited teachers for the nation's schools."[18] (193) The scholar Victor-Emmanuel Roberto Wilson provides great details about certain laws that were enacted during Christophe's kingdom and the King's impact on education in Haiti:

> Under Christophe, the North prospered. As a pragmatic administrator, Henry I promulgated the Code Henry, a civil code that established a sovereign court of justice (February 24, 1812), with 10 district courts and other small jurisdictions. He created the Military Penal Code, whose provisions were even more stringent than Dessalines' and which established Roman Catholicism as the official State Religion. The Code also provided for education by fostering private schools, given the lack of qualified teachers and, later, by bringing in foreign teachers for whom he funded the Royal Academy of Cap-Haïtien, which was then renamed Cap-Henry. Finally, a last decree established the Code Rural. Work was compulsory in Henry Christophe's kingdom; agriculture headed the list of priorities for the country's prosperity depended on it, according to the King.[19] (850)

Fils-Aimé points out that Christophe had a passion for education. There were several hundred schools all over his kingdom. He succeeded in making almost 30 percent of the population literate. Christophe created a university in his kingdom called l'Académie Royale in which Medicine, Fine Arts, Mathematics and Astronomy were taught. He also set up a printing press to produce the books needed to educate his people.[20] Christophe continued his work by restoring the Arsenal, investing in infrastructure and agriculture, which led his kingdom to prosperity:

> During the first few years of Christophe's reign, The Northern Plains were crisscrossed by plantations and trade flourished. Cap-Haïtien, founded in 1670 by French settlers, destroyed by fire February 7, 1802, to prevent the landing of an expeditionary force led by General Leclerc, Napoléon's brother-in-law, had been completely rebuilt. The gourd was established as official currency, backed by important gold reserves including coins bearing the King's portrait. In 1817, no less than 150 foreign vessels including many sailors under British and U.S. flags came to fill their holds with agricultural goods—coffee, sugar, tobacco, indigo, cocoa, molasses—providing the States' coffers with substantial profits. From 1811 to 1820, total exports from Haiti added up to more than 130 million pounds of various local commodities.[21] (Wilson 850)

In a discussion about King Christophe's legacy, the accomplishments mentioned above are worth mentioning.

Notes

[1] For example, he was originally a member of the communist party and in the fullness of time changed his position. Moreover, he talked about autonomy, yet he was in favor of keeping Martinique an overseas department of France.
[2] Fonkoua, Romuald. *Aimé Césaire (1913–2008)*. Perrin, 2010.
[3] Césaire, Aimé. *A Tempest*. Translated by Richard Miller. Theater Communications Group, 2002.
[4] Césaire, Aimé. *A Tempest*. Translated by Richard Miller. Theater Communications Group, 2022.

5. Christophe, Marc-A. "Totalitarianism and Authoritarianism in Aimé Césaire's 'La Tragédie du Roi Christophe.'" *CLA Journal*, September, 1978, Vol. 22, No. 1 (September, 1978), pp. 31–45.
6. This is a fictional account regarding King Christophe.
7. This is a factual account of King Christophe.
8. Christophe, Marc-A. "Totalitarianism and Authoritarianism in Aimé Césaire's 'La Tragédie du Roi Christophe.'" *CLA Journal*, September, 1978, Vol. 22, No. 1 (September, 1978), pp. 31–45.
9. Ibid., 38.
10. Moreau, Alain. "La démesure d'un héros grec, le roi Christophe." *Œuvres et Critiques* 18–19 (1993–1994) 281–290.
11. Christophe, Marc-A. "Totalitarianism and Authoritarianism in Aimé Césaire's 'La Tragédie du Roi Christophe.'" *CLA Journal*, September, 1978, Vol. 22, No. 1 (September, 1978), pp. 31–45.
12. Fuyet, Hervé, Nicole Fuyet, Guy Levilain and Mary Levilain. "Décolonisation et classes sociales dans La Tragédie du Roi Christophe d'Aimé Césaire." *The French Review*, May, 1973, Vol. 46, No. 6 (May, 1973), pp. 1101–1116.
13. Harris, Rodney E. Reviewed Work(s): "La tragédie du Roi Christophe by Aimé Césaire." *Books Abroad*, Vol. 45, No. 2 (Spring, 1971), p. 364.
14. Fils-Aimé, Jean. "La vérité sur Henri Christophe, le garçon de rue devenu le premier Roi d'Haïti." *Lumière sur le monde*. 2021 <https://www.youtube.com/watch?v=y_YvRn0ahGQ>
15. Ibid.
16. Destin, Yven. "Haiti's Prized Presidential Legacies." *Journal of Haitian Studies*, vol. 20, no. 2, 2014, pp. 191–207. *JSTOR*, <http://www.jstor.org/stable/24340374. Accessed 29 Aug. 2024>.
17. Ibid., 194.
18. Ibid., 193.
19. Wilson, Victor-Emmanuel Roberto, and Jacqueline Van Baelen. "The Forgotten Eighth Wonder of the World." *Callaloo*, vol. 15, no. 3, 1992, pp. 849–856. *JSTOR*, <https://doi.org/10.2307/2932028. Accessed 29 Aug. 2024>.
20. Fils-Aimé, Jean. "La vérité sur Henri Christophe, le garçon de rue devenu le premier Roi d'Haïti." *Lumière sur le monde*. 2021 <https://www.youtube.com/watch?v=y_YvRn0ahGQ>
21. Wilson, Victor-Emmanuel Roberto, and Jacqueline Van Baelen. "The Forgotten Eighth Wonder of the World." *Callaloo*, vol. 15, no. 3, 1992, pp. 849–856. *JSTOR*, <https://doi.org/10.2307/2932028. Accessed 29 Aug. 2024>.

Bibliography

Césaire, Aimé. *A Tempest*. Translated by Richard Miller. Theater Communications Group: New York, 2002.

———. *La tragédie du roi Christophe*. Présence Africaine: Paris 1963.

———. *La tragédie du roi Christophe*. Présence Africaine: Paris, 1970.

———. *The Tragedy of King Christophe*. Translated from the French by Paul Breslin and Rachel Ney. Northwestern University Press: Illinois, 2015.

Christophe, Marc-A. "Totalitarianism and Authoritarianism in Aimé Césaire's 'La Tragédie du Roi Christophe.'" *CLA Journal*, September, 1978, Vol. 22, No. 1 (September, 1978), pp. 31–45.

Coicou, Massillon. *Poésies nationales*. Imprimerie V. Goupy et Jourdain: Paris, 1892.

Destin, Yven. "Haiti's Prized Presidential Legacies." Journal of Haitian Studies, vol. 20, no. 2, 2014, pp. 191–207. JSTOR, <http://www.jstor.org/stable/24340374. Accessed 29 Aug. 2024>.

Fils-Aimé, Jean. "La vérité sur Henri Christophe, le garçon de rue devenu le premier Roi d'Haïti." Lumière sur le monde. 2021 <https://www.youtube.com/watch?v=y_YvRn0ahGQ>

Fonkoua, Romuald. *Aimé Césaire (1913–2008)*. Perrin, 2010.

Fuyet, Hervé, Nicole Fuyet, Guy Levilain and Mary Levilain. "Décolonisation et classes sociales dans La Tragédie du Roi Christophe d'Aimé Césaire." *The French Review*, May, 1973, Vol. 46, No. 6 (May, 1973), pp. 1101–1116.

Harris, Rodney E. Reviewed Work(s): "La tragédie du Roi Christophe by Aimé Césaire." *Books Abroad*, Vol. 45, No. 2 (Spring, 1971), p. 364.

Hoffmann, Léon-François. *Littérature d'Haïti*. Princeton, 1995.

Kennedy, Ellen Conroy. *The Negritude Poets: an Anthology of Translations from the French*. The Vikings Press, 1975.

Moreau, Alain. "La démesure d'un héros grec, le roi Christophe." *Œuvres et Critiques* 18–19 (1993–1994) 281–290.

Wilson, Victor-Emmanuel Roberto, and Jacqueline Van Baelen. "The Forgotten Eighth Wonder of the World." *Callaloo*, vol. 15, no. 3, 1992, pp. 849–856.

CHAPTER 3

The Esthetics of Protest: Jacques Roumain's Literary Indictment of the American Occupation of Haiti and the Haitian Catholic Church

Introduction

Jacques Roumain (1907–1944) was a prolific writer and one of the most renowned Haitian activist intellectuals of the twentieth century who questioned and confronted the American occupation, Western capitalism, secular humanism, and religion, in particular the Catholic clergy in Haiti. Although he later denounced his own bourgeois origins, he had the opportunity of studying and traveling in Europe and the United States, and when he returned to Haiti from Spain in 1927, he was deeply saddened to encounter a homeland still firmly under the rule of the United States marines. Under the pretext of restoring peace and stability, the U.S Marines invaded Haiti on July 28, 1915, and remained there until 1934. While much of Roumain's protest of the American occupation took form while the United States was still in power, nearly half a century later, the scholar Michael Dash posits a compelling summary of the aims of American politics with respect to Haiti at that time, in the following remarks:

> The spirit of the Monroe Doctrine was the ultimate rationale for control of the Caribbean. This had more to do with commercial expansion than with bringing enlightenment and democracy to Haiti. Indeed, well after the threat to hemispheric stability had passed with the end of the war in 1918, the Occupation continued.[1] (46–47)

Once on Haitian soil, United States Admiral Caperton through the use of coercive force and extortion, obtained the Haitian parliament's signature on the 1915 Convention by which the American forces would take control of the country. So, under pressure of circumstances, on September 16, 1915, the Foreign Minister Louis Borno (1865–1942), on behalf of the Haitian government, signed the Convention which ostensibly provided a legal basis to the occupation. Without delay, Admiral Caperton took over the country's military, legal and financial affairs.[2]

CHAPTER 3

The longstanding turmoil in Haiti provided a framework that shaped Roumain throughout his all too fleeting but momentous life. Over the course of time, animated by his profound patriotism, Jacques Roumain, a thought-provoking anthropologist, literary critic, poet, novelist, politician and activist, sought to address and undo certain social ills of Haiti's past, and he proposed a novel architecture for replacing them. In the decade of his life that he lived free of the American occupation prior to his Death, he purported a reimagined Catholic Church in Haiti, one that would not criminalize Voodoo practices as he saw them, but would incorporate science, and a paradigm shift in the clergy-parishioner hierarchy, particularly in the material differences between them. Through his writing and political activism, he encouraged the Haitian people to oppose the American occupation with the ultimate goal of dismantling it. A significant component of his suggested strategy for regaining control over the American occupiers and the eventual autonomy of the country involved pressing his fellow Haitians to preserve the roots of their African culture. He sought to diminish traces of the Americanization and Frenchification of Haitian identity and culture by reclaiming Haitians' African cultural heritage. This was a radical departure from previous Eurocentric postcolonial ideological legacy. Roumain's opposition to the mentality of eradication and obliteration of any remnant of African identity came to light through his attacks on the socio-economic consequences of colonialism as well as its concomitant proprietary spiritual relics. He felt that the application of a capitalist democracy imposed on the Haitian nation had and would continue to irretrievably cause further harm to the poor while boosting the dominion of the ruling class.

This study will analyze Jacques Roumain's reactions to the American occupation of Haiti, and I will examine his contribution to the fight against anti-superstition campaigning, a hallmark of the Catholic Church in Haiti at the time. For this latter point, I shall discuss his poem *"Nouveau Sermon Nègre"* because it crystallizes Roumain's philosophical dispute against one of the institutions with which he often found fault, the Catholic Church.

It is worthy of note that much Roumain scholarship tends to focus on a definition of his approach to dissent that relies on a specific foundation of his background as opposed to addressing the different genres in which he wrote and the varied topics that he explored. However, this study will consider Roumain's esthetics of protest by examining multiple examples of his oeuvre: several articles and a poem which, taken together, served his message of promoting Haitian sovereignty in consistent, coherent and harmonious manifestations. My analysis will reveal the common Roumain denominator of his outrage over the lack of a greater public remonstration against all types of assault on Haitian identity and self-determination. His critique of society comprised his firm belief that the failure to denounce the mistreatment of Haitians made people complicit in it. The works that I discuss encompass a decade and a half, and Roumain's commitment to the promotion of the ideals and implementation of a Haiti in alignment with his vision, never wavered. This integrity of ideals is manifest in spite of beatings, torture and multiple imprisonments (Gaillard 1)[3] (Dorsinville 67)[4] (Jean 7–8)[5].

The American Occupation of Haiti

Aware of the political, literary and philosophical ideas of his time, at an early age, Roumain exhibited the degree of his willingness to become, and later remain, a resounding voice in the fight for social justice and change. In 1925 (at 18 years of age), while studying abroad, according to Roumain biographer Carolyn Fowler, he expressed his desire to return home in order to actively participate in the liberation of his country in "a letter to Joseph Jolibois Fils, director of the Opposition newspaper *Courrier Haitien* and acknowledged Nationalist leader"[6] (Fowler 7) Over the next two years, Jacques Roumain and his colleagues took part in an intellectual resistance in an attempt to fight effectively against the American occupation of Haiti. In fact, in 1927, within the same year as his arrival to Haiti, together with his Haitian colleagues Philippe Thoby-Marcelin, Carl Brouard, Emile Roumer, Normil Sylvain, Daniel Heurtelou, and Antonio Vieux, Roumain founded *La Revue Indigène*,[7] a monthly Haitian journal whose mission was to fight Western materialism, promote Haitian culture, and illuminate the significance of African heritage in Haitian culture. In *La Revue Indigène* (July 1929), they made it their goal to build an original doctrine, use art to foster a sense of community, fight against misconceptions, establish a strong ethical code, and become familiar with Latin American literature. With his continued efforts and constant engagement, Roumain was able to expose some of the ruses used by the occupiers to carry out their agenda. He specifies these in articles which I discuss later.

Some of the factors that contributed to shaping Roumain's evocative and effective arguments against the American occupation and later the Catholic Church in Haiti can be traced to an optic proposed by Jean Price-Mars (1876–1969). In his book originally published as *Ainsi Parla l'Oncle* and translated as *So Spoke the Uncle* (1928), Price-Mars identified the African influence on Haitians and urged Haitians to embrace their African heritage. This perspective clearly did not propagate a Europeanization of Haitian identity, and in fact was a way of reclaiming Haitian ancestry. The return to the authentic, the essential, in contrast to the manufactured identity is a central theme in Roumain's protests and can be seen across various genres. There was also a linguistic contour to his aesthetic of protest. It is worthy of note that according to the scholar Marie-José Nzengou-Tayo, "under the tutelage of Jean Price-Mars (1876–1969) and Georges Sylvain (1866–1925), Haitian intellectuals became aware that the culture and language of peasants could help in rallying them against the occupying Americans."[8] (153) Therefore, by sharing, embracing and applying Price-Mars' ideology, Roumain spoke on behalf of marginalized Haitians. Moreover, Roumain's focus on agrarian life and the rural landscape made him infinitely relatable because he evoked Haitian essence on its own terms as opposed to having any external imposition define what it meant to be a citizen of Haiti. Clearly these were welcome changes, so, it is not surprising that he was one of the most beloved figures of his generation.

Roumain's influence has been well documented by literary critics. Interestingly, different critics emphasize distinctive aspects of Roumain's biography and creations. The scholar Jean-Claude Michel, in realizing the impact of Roumain in Haitian literature, mentions that,

> For most of those indigenist writers also, poetry was not a privileged diversion, but a means of discovery, of communication and of action… This poetry, deeply marked by Marxist theories, praised all at once with romanticism: the proletarian fraternity, the universal value of social justices, and the particular values of negritude. Roumain is the one who expressed better this new awakening of conscience.[9] (130–131)

The critic Marc Roland Thadal points out that Roumain's articles were used to energize the masses and *"réveiller la conscience nationale."*[10] (13–14) Frantz-Antoine Leconte observes how Roumain was proposing a new order that was organized and viable. "Roumain's text, beyond its literary success, transcends the reassuring neutrality to become a writing of testimony, of fight, of contestation and of condemnation of the drifts and disasters of a society which is nevertheless organizable."[11] (7) The celebrated Haitian historian and novelist Roger Gaillard observes that in addition to Roumain's literary works, he also organized strikes, particularly among Haiti's youth: "He has been to prison twice, and multiple youth organizations owe their validity to him then. He is already a 'leader'."[12] (Gaillard 1)

Any time there was an event that exerted a negative impact on the daily lives of his compatriots, Roumain used his writing to express his concerns, and his protests against the authoritative forces were remarkable. Through strikes, articles, and poems, he made the authorities aware in no uncertain terms, that the voices of the masses must be heard and their conditions must be changed. I will examine his article *"Autour de la taxe sur l'alcool et le tabac"* (1928) and the book *"Analyse schématique"* (1934) in order to elucidate Roumain's perspective on the occupation. In these two works, Roumain delivered articulate arguments against the occupation and provided suggestions to bring about radical changes.

In his article *"Autour de la taxe sur l'alcool et le tabac,"* published in the Haitian newspaper *Le Petit Impartial* on September 29, 1928, Roumain highlighted the methodical rapaciousness of the members of the Taxation Office for reorganizing the tax code to benefit the rich and American occupancy while inflicting untold damage on the vast majority of Haitians. He underlined that, while many small businesses were closing, unemployment was rising, and members of the working class were starving, the government imposed a tax on alcohol. On August 14, 1928, the Excise Tax Law[13] was passed that taxed alcohol consumption destined for local production, but not that which was intended for exportation. This law negatively impacted Haitian rural workers in particular, but essentially all subjugated workers, because it was designed to demoralize them by restricting their ability to spend their extremely limited disposable income on any form of leisure while at the same time causing them to work harder to earn that meager amount of money. Roumain saw this as a decisive step toward further domination and was furious that people did not rise up to protest such a decree.

> *Et personne n'a protesté, et tout le monde continue à encourager par un silence inexplicable le dépècement méthodique de notre Patrie par les vautours yankees ! Après la dépossession illégale des paysans impuissants et désarmés, le Conseiller Financier continue son œuvre de mort en ruinant, bien couvert par les lois du traître Borno et la force militaire, nos rares industries nationales, préparant ainsi le terrain à l'envahissement progressif du pays par le Capital américain.*[14] (Œuvres complètes, 500)

> And nobody protested, and everybody continues to encourage by an inexplicable silence the methodical deprivation of our Fatherland by the Yankee vultures! After the illegal dispossession of the helpless and unarmed peasants, the Financial Adviser continues his work of Death by ruining, well covered by the laws of the traitor Borno and the military force, our few national industries, thus preparing the ground for the progressive invasion of the country by the American Capital.

Roumain considered that the totality of the laws proposed by the Americans and adopted by the Haitian government, were designed to put Haiti in economic and financial servitude while benefiting the Americans. As such, he made a call to all Haitians to stand up in order to defend their nation against the American occupation.

According to the scholar Hérold Toussaint, there was an array of calculating unscrupulous methods that the occupiers used to seize and try to perpetuate control of the country. Taking extreme advantage of Haitian peasants was one of them, and nowhere is this more apparent than the relentless assault on land ownership rights. Toussaint commented on the ravages of these abuses by stating thus,

> *Quant aux expropriations, c'est la nouvelle Constitution de 1918 qui va leur servir de rempart. Au nom de la loi, un bon nombre de petits et de moyens paysans furent expulsés de leurs terres. Les clauses de plusieurs contrats ne purent être remplies sans déloger un certain nombre de paysans. Comme certains paysans étaient incapables de prouver leurs titres de propriété, les autorités pouvaient se servir de la loi pour leur déposséder. Une telle pratique—les expropriations—provoqua une massive émigration des paysans haïtiens vers Port-au-Prince ou la République dominicaine.*[15] (86)

As for the expropriations, it was the new Constitution of 1918 that served as a bulwark against them. In the name of the law, a good number of strapped and distressed peasants were expelled from their land. The clauses of several contracts could not be fulfilled without dislodging a number of peasants. As some peasants were unable to prove their title of land ownership, the authorities could use the law to dispossess them. This practice of expropriation led to a massive emigration of Haitian peasants to Port-au-Prince or the Dominican Republic.

There can be no doubt that there was a formidable financial motive in American domination. In discussing the American occupation, Makouta-Mboukou mentions that: "The real motive for U.S. intervention in these regions [in America] is that the United States, having reached the imperialist stage of its economic Development, seeks to secure for its capital and investments the maximum guarantee and profit."[16] (52) For Roumain, the assault on Haitian self-determination, which exhibited egregious financial and psychosocial dynamics, needed to be contested by combining literature and politics in order to unify Haitians, and thus defend their country collectively. He expressed his anger in writing or through protests any time he saw "Haitian governments whose policies betrayed Haitian interests to those of the American occupation."[17] (Cobb 90) According to Roger Dorsinville, in 1929, Jacques Roumain was arrested many times. One of the reasons: "… he received leaflets from abroad. He was accused of receiving weapons, and even of having a plan of the National Palace to facilitate the assassination of the President. He was brought before a court martial, tried and convicted."[18] (67) Eddy Arnold Jean mentioned other reasons why he was arrested that year: "In 1929, Roumain was thrown into prison for leading student strikes and setting fire to the current Cine-Paramount … Released, he was incarcerated once again because of his virulent articles against the government and its lackeys. This time he was sentenced to three years in prison."[19] (7–8) Therefore, Roumain's objective of writing as a form of consciousness raising, and a catalyst to change was deemed threatening enough to the status quo that the people in power tried to silence him. It is worthy of note that these attempts at censoring him were singularly futile since Roumain was so determined to free his country that pressure, beatings and incarcerations did not deter him.

Seven years after his article protesting the Excise Tax Law, in 1934, the committee of the Haitian Communist Party, of which Roumain was a member, published a sociopolitical study called *Analyse chématique*. In it, Roumain laid out some of the reasons why Haitians were protesting the American occupation of Haiti: "Le Nationalisme haïtien est né de la corvée[20] rétablie dans nos campagnes par les troupes d'invasion ; du massacre de plus de 3.000 paysans haïtiens protestataires ; de l'expropriation des paysans par les grandes compagnies américaines." "Haitian Nationalism was born from the corvée reestablished in our countryside by the invading troops; from the massacre of more than 3,000 protesting Haitian peasants; from the expropriation of the peasants by the large American companies." (*Œuvres complètes*, 653). The struggle Roumain engaged in was not only against imperialism and capitalism, it was also against the Haitian bourgeoisie and politicians working for foreign imperialists in order to exploit peasants and vulnerable workers (*Œuvres complètes*, 655). He condemned their compliance with the occupants in order to obtain high level positions in the government.

> *La bourgeoisie haïtienne tandis qu'on massacrait les paysans du Nord, de l'Artibonite et du Plateau Central, recevait joyeusement les chefs des assassins dans les salons de ses cercles mondains et dans ses familles. Complice consciente de l'Occupation, elle se mit à son service, rampa aux pieds des maîtres en quête de reliefs : présidence de la République, fonctions publiques.* (*Œuvres complètes*, 635)

> The Haitian bourgeoisie, while the peasants of the North, the Artibonite and the Central Plateau were being massacred, joyfully received the leaders of the assassins in the salons of their social circles and in their families. Conscious accomplice of the Occupation, it put itself at its service, crawled at the feet of the masters in search of reliefs: presidency of the Republic, public functions.

After co-founding the Communist Party in 1934 in Haiti: "That same year, Roumain was arrested by Vincent's demagogue government and sentenced to two years in prison. His sentence expunged, Roumain had to go into exile."[21] (Jean 8) Exile clearly occupied a central role in Roumain's esthetics of poetic protest. The eminent Haitian historian and intellectual Hénock Trouillot published a critical biography on Jacques Roumain in 1981, and in it, he mentions that exile and the Spanish Civil War[22] (1936–1939), had a significant impact on Roumain's conception of poetry: "Ainsi après son exil, après la transformation doctrinale de sa pensée en 1934, Jacques Roumain entendait renouveler sa poétique, la charger de revendications, d'une partie du bouleversement mondial, des souffrances ou des révoltes humaines. Il s'est par là profondément transformé"[23] (Trouillot 132–133) "Thus after his exile, after the doctrinal transformation of his thought in 1934, Jacques Roumain intended to renew his poetics, to charge them with claims, with a part of the world upheaval, with human sufferings or revolts. He was by there deeply transformed." (132–133). This modification in his outlook became a permanent part of the Roumain poetic repertoire since in a speech entitled *"La poésie comme arme"* delivered by Jacques Roumain in Cuba in 1940, he mentions that: *"Le poète est à la fois témoin et acteur du drame historique. Il y est enrôlé avec sa pleine responsabilité. Et particulièrement dans notre temps, son art doit être une arme de première ligne au service de son peuple."* "The poet is at the same time witness and actor of the historical drama. He is enrolled in it with his full responsibility. And especially in our time, his art must be a front-line weapon in the service of his people."[24] (*"La poésie comme arme"* 40) This protest manifests in his position toward the Catholic Church.

Roumain's Fight Against the Anti-superstition Campaign

Starting under the Regine of President Sténio Vincent, the Catholic Church spearheaded what they called an "anti-superstition campaign." Superstition in this instance referred to the collection of religious beliefs and practices that emanated from Africa. One of the Catholic Church's most direct ways to launch an attack on perceived superstition was, according to Leconte, to destroy Voodoo temples and threaten any Voodoo practitioners with excommunication.[25] (Leconte 199) Leconte states that this was carried out in agreement with the government of Élie Lescot. According to Toussaint, this campaign was seen as a vast purge whose purpose was to: *"extirper le vaudou du sol haïtien, détruire tout objet qui se rapporte au culte vaudou."* "Extirpate Voodoo from Haitian soil, destroy any object that relates to the Voodoo cult."[26] (110) Toussaint further states that not unsurprisingly, Voodoo was considered the symbol of barbarism, and in fact was compared to leprosy. (111) Toussaint theorizes that Jacques Roumain regarded this anti-superstition campaign as a diversionary tactic to simultaneously divide Haitians, and avoid the real social problems facing them such as poor health, illiteracy and poverty.[27] (115) Roumain felt that it was his duty to defend and advocate for the impoverished as well as their religious preferences and practices. *"Fils de grands propriétaires terriens, j'ai renié mes origines bourgeoises. J'ai beaucoup vécu avec les paysans. Je connais leur vie, leur mentalité, leur religion-ce mélange étonnant de catholicisme et de vaudou."* "Son of large landowners, I disavowed my bourgeois origins. I have lived a lot with the peasants. I know their life, their mentality, their religion-an astonishing mixture of Catholicism and Voodoo." (*Œuvres complètes*, 639).

Since Roumain's message cannot be thoroughly deciphered without taking into consideration the Haitian cultural context from which it emerged, it is worthwhile reexamining some of his ideas as well as those of Haitian and non-Haitian Roumain scholars who wrote about them. Scholar Lewis A. Clorméus wrote a superb article entitled « Des leaders protestants haïtiens dans la vague anticléricale et nationaliste (1927–1929) » on Roumain's anticlerical involvement in the late 1920s, which helps to contextualize this conflict of the 1940s. Roumain was extremely apprehensive about foreign missionaries because he held that they were perpetuating the same identity vandalism as the American occupation, which favored a Eurocentric model imposed onto the Haitian people. In Roumain's words, "*Ces religieux qui vous font imbécilement ânonner 'Nos ancêtres les Gaulois', qui vous donnent une éducation toute française et font de vous moins des Haïtiens que des caricatures de Français, vous détestent, vous exploitent et vous méprisent.*" (*Œuvres complètes*, 502–503) "These religious people who stupidly make you say 'Our ancestors the Gauls', who give you an all-French education and make you not so much Haitians as caricatures of the French, hate you, exploit you and despise you." (*Œuvres complètes*, 502–503). He decried the collaboration of the clergy with the Haitian government run by the occupancy by denouncing the fact that foreign bishops were illegally nominated in the place of Haitian priests. (*Œuvres complètes*, 517) Roumain felt that the true agenda of the Catholic Church was to disparage Voodoo so much that it would be replaced by Catholicism. Destroying the religion of the masses, would, in principle, facilitate converting Haitians to Catholicism and thus in all likelihood would also expedite adoption of European culture. It was, moreover, a way to ensure renouncing and perhaps eventually abandoning Afro-centered identity. In 1978, the prolific Congolese literary scholar and historian Jean-Pierre Makouta-Mboukou published a landmark study on Jacques Roumain's engagement with religion, *Jacques Roumain: Essai sur la signification spirituelle et religieuse de son oeuvre*. In that work, Makouta-Mboukou concurs with Roumain as the former comments on the campaign in the following remarks: "*un processus d'acculturation, qui a pour fin ultime, non le salut de l'homme au sens biblique, mais une assimilation totale c'est-à-dire une occidentalisation.*"[28] "A process of acculturation, which has as its ultimate goal, not the salvation of man in the biblical sense, but a total assimilation, that is to say a westernization." (83)

Before analyzing "*Nouveau Sermon Nègre*," in which Roumain poetically reappropriates the teachings of Christ, it is useful to examine his articles "*À propos de la campagne anti-superstitieuse*" (1942/1944) and "*Réplique finale au Révérend Père*

Foisset" (1942), published in *Le Nouvelliste*. They are crucial to forging a deeper understanding of Roumain's radical critique of the Catholic Church and institutionalized Christianity in Haiti and are vociferously echoed in *"Nouveau Sermon Nègre."* Jacques Roumain wrote three articles entitled *"Sur les superstitions"* on March 11, 13, and 19, 1942. This title was later modified to be called, *"À propos de la campagne 'anti-superstitieuse' /Las Supersticiones."*

In these articles, Roumain stated that he did not envision Voodoo as superstition, but rather as a Catholic-Voodoo syncretism. He criticized the clergy for misunderstanding and mischaracterizing the Haitian peasants, and the issues afflicting them. He mentions that: *"L'Haïtien n'est pas plus-ni moins-superstitieux qu'un autre peuple. Les pratiques dites superstitieuses auxquelles il se livre ont un caractère universel."* "The Haitian is not more or less superstitious than any other people. The so-called superstitious practices in which he indulges have a universal character." (*Œuvres complètes*, 745–746) He furnished examples of universal superstitions from countries such as France, Italy, Germany, Syria, and Australia, and expounded that these practices are similar to the ones that can be found in Voodoo. This research formed the basis for his concept that Voodoo and Catholicism were not mutually exclusive and, in fact, were intertwined.

> *Le Clergé lui-même a contribué à maintenir la croyance en la présence des loas[29] : en les combattant comme une réalité redoutable, en abattant par exemple certains arbres sous prétexte d'en chasser les mauvais esprits : ce qui, pour les paysans, passait pour la confirmation évidente de leur existence.* (*Œuvres complètes*, 750).

> The clergy itself contributed to maintaining the belief in the presence of the loas: by fighting them as a fearsome reality, by cutting down for example certain trees under the pretext of chasing away the evil spirits: which, for the peasants, passed for the obvious confirmation of their existence.

Roumain maintained that the religious issues professed by many religious leaders and the Haitian government were not the crucial issues facing Haitian peasants. He understood that Haitian peasants could benefit from help, but that an injudicious and erroneous approach was used in an attempt to steer them in a more favorable direction:

> *Il faut naturellement débarrasser la masse haïtienne de ses entraves mystiques. Mais on ne triomphera pas de ses croyances par la violence ou en la menaçant de l'enfer. Ce n'est pas la hache du bourreau, la flamme du bûcher, les autodafés qui ont détruit la sorcellerie. C'est le progrès de la science, le développement continu de la culture humaine, une connaissance chaque jour plus approfondie de la structure de l'Univers.* (*Œuvres complètes*, 750)

> Naturally, it is necessary to rid the Haitian mass of its mystical fetters. But one will not triumph over its beliefs by violence or by threatening it with hell. It is not the ax of the executioner, the flame of the stake, the autodafés that have destroyed witchcraft. It is the progress of science, the continuous Development of human culture, a knowledge each day more profound of the structure of the Universe.

Roumain expressed his frustration about the insufficiency and the ineffectiveness of the clergy when it came to social practices, which he believed were part of their professed religious practices. He maintained that as long as there were not enough rural clinics for peasants, as long as the peasants had no funds to pay for adequate healthcare, they would consult the Voodoo priests when they became ill. He also lamented the Haitian Catholic Church's indifference toward the socio-economic realities in which their parishioners lived. He believed that, in order to really change the mentality of Haitian peasants, the government as well as the religious leaders must create an environment in which the Haitian peasant could truly evolve. This meant that peasants must have access to an education; their material condition and standard of living must be improved, and that there should be an infrastructure in place allowing them to live well. The Catholic priests possessed adequate means to be cared for in proper hospitals themselves, but the peasants were left to struggle. That is why Roumain rightfully argues that:

> Ce qu'il faut mener en Haïti, ce n'est pas une campagne antisuperstitieuse, mais une campagne anti-misère. Avec l'école, l'hygiène, un standard de vie plus élevé, le paysan aura accès à cette culture et à cette vie décente qu'on ne peut lui refuser, si on ne veut pas que ce pays tout entier périsse, et qui lui permettront de surmonter des survivances religieuses enracinées dans sa misère, son ignorance, son exploitation séculaires. (Œuvres complètes, 751).

> What is needed in Haiti is not an anti-superstition campaign, but an anti-misery campaign. With schooling, hygiene, a higher standard of living, the peasant will have access to that culture and that decent life which cannot be denied him, if we do not want this whole country to perish, and which will allow him to overcome religious survivals rooted in his misery, his ignorance, his age-old exploitation.

The Haitian scholar Celucien L. Joseph wrote the most comprehensive intellectual biography on Jacques Roumain in the English language: *Thinking in Public: Faith, Secular Humanism, and Development in Jacques Roumain* (2017) and contributed vital articles on Roumain's engagement with religion. According to him, Roumain remained convinced that the Church betrayed what was purported to be its mission as "an instrument of social change and practical democracy."[30] (Joseph 248–249) Furthermore, Roumain argued that the priests could carry out a more meaningful mission by tending to social projects that involved the creation of schools as part of the overall mission of educating the disenfranchised, building hospitals and creating jobs, particularly in the Haitian countryside.[31] (Joseph 248–249) In a particularly subtle feature of Joseph's research on Roumain's complex relationship to organized religion, Joseph argues that the activist was against the repressions and hierarchies that he observed[32] (Joseph 251), because he only endorsed organized religion that promoted positive and enduring social transformation.

Roumain's work entitled *"Réplique finale au Révérend Père Foisset"* is significant because it was a public forum and therefore would reach many readers. After Jacques Roumain's articles against the anti-superstition campaign were published, Father Foisset, a French priest, answered with a series of articles published in *La Phalange*, the official Haitian Catholic Newspaper between February 25 and June 18, 1942. These letters prompted Roumain to respond, and this exchange sparked an intellectual correspondence between the two men. According to Joseph, Roumain was incensed because "Foisset approved the assault and the persecution of the adherents of the vodou faith."[33] (244) The exchanges between the two men provided a platform for Roumain to make his case for the Haitian peasants, their right to a better life and freedom of religious choice and beliefs. Celucien L. Joseph argues that according to Roumain: "Catholicism was no better for the peasants than Vaudou" (244). During these heated exchanges between the two writers, Roumain mentions *"Il n'a répondu, il n'a pu répondre, à aucune de mes réfutations… parce qu'il est incapable de me contredire."* "He has not responded, he could not respond, to any of my rebuttals … because he is incapable of contradicting me." (Œuvres complètes, 776) Roumain listed a number of areas in which he had consequential differences with the Catholic Church:

> *Quand un prêtre monte en chaire, comme cela est arrivé récemment, pour affirmer que la pluie et une bonne récolte sont la conséquence d'une conversion du vaudou-catholicisme au catholicisme pur, il reprend l'héritage du Houngan*[34] *qui en cas de sécheresse recommande un service de loa.*[35] (Œuvres complètes, 780)

> When a priest climbs to the pulpit, as happened recently, to assert that rain and a good harvest are the consequence of a conversion from Voodoo-Catholicism to pure Catholicism, he is taking up the heritage of the Houngan who in case of drought recommends a loa service.

Roumain the activist and Roumain the anthropologist converged in a unified protest denouncing both the clergy as well as their exploits in the following manner: *"Mais j'appelle fripons en toutes lettres (et je peux citer des noms) les prêtres qui ont pris prétexte de la campagne antisuperstitieuse pour voler des pièces ethnographiques, historiques, et archéologiques, malgré les prescriptions formelles du Décret-Loi du 31 octobre 1941."* "But I call scoundrels in full (and I can name names) the priests who took pretexts of the anti-superstitious campaign to steal ethnographic, historical, and archaeological pieces, despite the formal prescriptions of the Decree-Law of October 31, 1941." (*Œuvres complètes*, 788) Although he acknowledged the accomplishments of some priests who worked assiduously to help change the lives of their parishioners, he reproached priests who lived in mansions when their places of worship were in deplorable states of physical deterioration. (*Œuvres complètes*, 791). He was opposed to people who used religion as a means of division, and he points this out in a forceful example: *"Non, quand un prêtre fait du crucifix une matraque et de la croix du Seigneur la croix gammée du Führer, il ne mérite qu'une chose : notre souverain mépris."* "No, when a priest turns the crucifix into a baton and the Lord's cross into the Führer's swastika, he deserves only one thing: our sovereign contempt." (*Œuvres complètes*, 791). On the other hand, he did see ways in which people could cast their political and religious ideologies aside in order to really work together effectively to solve what he defined as the pressing problems of the times such as *"le chômage, la guerre, la lutte antifasciste, la liberté, la justice, le droit à une vie décente pour toute l'humanité."* "unemployment, war, the anti-fascist struggle, freedom, justice, the right to a decent life for all humanity." (*Œuvres complètes*, 792) In addition, he reproached the narrowmindedness of Father Foisset.

The Catholic Church in Haiti, whose hierarchy came from France, greeted the American occupation of Haiti with optimism because it saw a stalwart ally in the occupation.[36] That is why, according to Toussaint, Roumain expressed his condemnation in the following manner: "to reproach most members of the clergy for their contempt for Haitian culture, to clarify the link between Voodoo and socio-economic conditions in Haiti, to advocate social and economic transformation in Haiti."[37] (Toussaint 125) Other Haitian scholars, such as Celucien L. Joseph, also contributed to the discussion of the intersection of Roumain's anticlericalism, the criminalization of Voodoo, and the American occupation:

> Roumain's seemingly anticlericalism during the period of the American occupation was an inevitable response to the cooperative Church with the American occupants to subdue the Haitian people to the imperial forces, and to demonize Vodou practitioners to renounce the religion of their ancestors in favor of imperial Christianity. The Church of the American occupation contributed substantially to the criminalization of Vodou and its associated practices.[38] (17)

Roumain's condemnation of the Catholic Church's attacks on what it classified as superstition coincided with his criticism of the Haitian government for failing to invest enough in the peasantry and for not seeing and denouncing the ravages of unbridled capitalism.[39] Therefore, because of Roumain's challenge to the United States Occupation of Haiti and his involvement in Haiti's politics, it is accurate to state that he was in constant conflict with the Haitian government. In commenting on the Roumain juxtaposition of religion and politics, Joseph theorizes that "He [Roumain] underscores Christianity's role (or support of) in subjugating weak peoples, pacifying them, and conquering less-powerful nations."[40] (247) Furthermore, Roumain's Christ is a kindred revolutionary of sorts.[41] (252) Rather than exclude social Development from the religious discussion, Joseph points out that for Roumain, social Development should form an integral part of the religious discussion: "Jacques Roumain was not particularly concerned about the abstract dimension or theories of religion but on what religion can and should do to improve the human condition and to make the world a better place."[42] (258)

The mistreatment of Roumain by the Haitian government did not diminish his resolve to be a catalyst for change to promote Haitian culture and speak on behalf of the underprivileged. In 1941, the Haitian government entrusted Roumain with the management of the newly created Bureau d'Éthnologie, created by the decree-law of October 31, 1941. He also published many scientific papers about Haiti and its people.[43] In 1943, in Mexico, where he worked as *chargé d'affaires*[44] under President Élie Lescot, he completed the poetry collection *Bois-d'ébène (Ebony Wood)*. One of his most acclaimed poems, "Nouveau Sermon Nègre" which I will analyze below, is from this volume.

Analysis of "Nouveau Sermon Nègre"

Francophone Caribbean poetry often depicts the theme of religion, and since the people's relationship to religion is fraught with complexity, the literary material that is produced as a result is quite rich. Historically, the Africans that were brought over as slaves in the Caribbean were forcibly converted to Christianity. According to the historian Marcus W. Jernegan, "The French *Code Noir* of 1685 obliged every planter to have his Negroes baptized and properly instructed in the doctrines and duties of Christianity."[45] (505) One aspect of tactics utilized by the oppressors to motivate slaves to accept their horrific situation involved the hope and promise of a glorious afterlife via salvation. An additional weapon was the threat of denial of an eternity in heaven in the event that slaves broke away from the newly proposed status quo. This method presents an example of a particularly effective form of brainwashing as it was based on sinister intentions. In *The Wretched of the Earth* Frantz Fanon (1925–1961), the renowned Martinican intellectual and psychiatrist offered an interpretation of how this brainwashing came about:

> The colonialist bourgeoisie is aided and abetted in the pacification of the colonized by the inescapable powers of religion. All the saints who turned the other cheek, who forgave those who trespassed against them, who, without flinching, were spat upon and insulted, are championed and shown as an example.[46] (28)

Jacques Roumain did not subscribe to this type of misconstrued application of the teachings of the gospel. He was not alone in believing that this kind of distorted behavior was unacceptable and should be addressed and rectified. In referring to some of the writers of the Caribbean islands and their political works, the critic G. R. Coulthard points out:

> Another avenue of attack on European civilization consists in a criticism of Christianity, in its relation to the Negro world. The line taken is a fairly obvious one that Christianity is a white man's religion at best, closing its eyes to racial discrimination, indifferent to the oppression and persecution of the Negro, and at worst an active agent of colonialism helping to keep the Negro in subjugation.[47] (239)

Such unrelenting efforts toward annihilating the identity of those of another race by imposing their own is one reason why many Caribbean writers express reservations about Christianity.[48]

Roumain's poem, "*Nouveau Sermon Nègre*," which illustrates his desire to break from the existing institution of the Church and establish an alternative approach, accents the theme of self-determination. The choice of the word "nouveau" challenges the reader to consider the "old" Negro Sermon. The opening lines of the poem provide a glimpse of the prevailing sermon, one in which certain interpretations of the Bible not only defile Blacks but also Christ himself. Roumain draws parallels between the hardships of Blacks and the suffering of Christ. He writes "*Nouveau Sermon Nègre*," free from the duplicity of the Church, as a sermon that is not only endogenous, but also in line with the virtues of Christ, whom he saw as a noble revolutionary. According to Ellen Conroy Kennedy, scholar and translator of some of Roumain's poems into English:

> The poem's title shows that Roumain ... was an admirer of James Weldon Johnson, particularly his poetic re-creation of old-time New Negro Sermon in *God's Trombones*, first published in 1927. Roumain's sermon is "new" by virtue of being written from outside the Christian faith rather than from within, and because it appears to be a direct response to Johnson's. If Johnson's sermons were encouragements to follow the way of the Lord, exhortations against sin but resignation as to its workings, Roumain's is a protest against the betrayal of Christian ideals by the institutionalized Church and an exhortation to revolt.[49] (20)

In this poem, composed of free verse and divided into four stanzas of uneven length, Roumain unveils the hypocrisy of Church leaders as well as the alliance of the wealthy in order to further crush and alienate the poor. His firm stance against injustice and his desire for drastic change are fully expressed. The opening lines of the poem justify the necessity of a new Negro sermon:

> *Ils ont craché à Sa Face leur mépris glacé*
> *Comme un drapeau noir flotte au vent battu par la neige*
> *Pour faire de lui le pauvre nègre, le dieu des puissants*[50]

> They spat their cool contempt in his face
> Like a Black flag waving in the wind beaten by snow
> To make of him the poor negro the God of the powerful

In the first line, the poet uses capital letters in the possessive adjective "Sa" and the noun "Face" to accentuate the two words on which he intends to focus. The same line repeats the use of the vowel "a" four times: "craché," "à," "Sa," "Face." This assonance expresses the open and vivid sound associated with anger, thus corresponding to a mad person's spitting of saliva on someone else's face. Such a gesture expresses disrespect, disdain, and hatred. Roumain makes clear that the face they spat on is that of Christ. This description asserts that those who did so acted maliciously. This imagery portrays "ils" "they" who spit as white. The suggestion here seems to be that the whites (possibly white institutions) have taken Christ and rendered him unrecognizable, like a Black flag turned white by snow. Here, we see the parallel between Christ and Black people who have been covered by white institutions. Both Christ and Blacks have been exploited to the point that they are unrecognizable, to the point that their true color or zeal has been coated by the gusting power of white institutions, like flags windswept by snow. Therefore, Christ is a victim of the same institutional powers that maintain Blacks in bondage. In this way, his experience mirrors the Black experience. Both Christ and Blacks are used and abused by those in power. Roumain highlights the irony of the existence of people who call themselves Christians and yet act more similarly to the people who denied Christ's status as the Messiah and then tortured and killed him.

The next verses show how a humble Christ has been maneuvered just as Blacks have, to reinforce institutional power.

> *De ses haillons des ornements d'autel*
> *De son doux chant de misère*
> *De sa plainte tremblante de banjo*
> *Le tumulte orgueilleux de l'orgue*
> *De ses bras qui halaient les lourds chalands*

sur le fleuve Jourdain
L'arme de ceux qui frappent par l'épée
De son corps épuisé comme le nôtre dans les plantations
                                            de coton[51]

Of his rags the vestments of the altar
Of his muted chant of misery
Of the trembling wail of his banjo
The arrogant din of the organ
Of his arms that pulled the heavy barges
On the river Jordan
The weapon of those who live by the sword
Of his body like ours wasted on the cotton
                                            plantations

The lines above show how white institutions changed the discussion on the nature of Jesus to the point that he becomes someone completely different. The vocabulary of poverty and suffering usually associated with Jesus and expressed through words like "*Haillons*," "rags," "*plainte tremblante*" "trembling wail," and "banjo" is substituted with "ornements" "vestments," "tumulte orgueilleux" "arrogant din" and "orgue" "organ." The simplicity of Jesus' nature is replaced with lavish and sophisticated decorations. The traditional musical instrument "banjo," seen as an inferior instrument, is replaced with the "orgue," which is a classical music instrument associated with prestige, riches, and with Church music. The connection between the exploitation of Christ and Blacks is heightened by Roumain's description not of a heavenly Christ, but of the man who walked the earth in "*haillons*"[52] "rags." The imagery used to refer to Christ forces the reader to consider the parallel manipulation between Christ and that which occurred during colonial slavery.[53] Roumain uses vagueness in his depiction in order to switch seamlessly between the image of Christ and that of Black people. The line "*De ses haillons des ornements d'autel*"[54] "of his rags the vestments of the altar" appears to refer to Christ, yet "*De ses bras qui halaient les lourds chalands*"[55] "of his arms that pulled the heavy barges" makes suggestion of plantations. The quick geographical clarification on the next line where the pulling took place, "*Sur le fleuve Jourdain*"[56] "On the Jordan river" confirms that the subject is in fact Christ. Yet Roumain pushes forward his allegorical imagery between the African slaves and Christ, stating "*De son corps épuisé comme le nôtre dans les plantations de coton.*"[57] "of his body wasted on the cotton plantation." At this point, Roumain assertively describes the exploitive process of both subjects. He seems to have no regret or hesitation in his analogy.

An appeal from Roumain to Christ, presumably on behalf of all Blacks, follows:

Tel un charbon ardent
Tel un charbon ardent dans un buisson de roses blanches
le bouclier d'or de leur fortune
Ils ont blanchi Sa Face noire sous le crachat de leur
mépris glacé

Ils ont craché sur Ta Face noire
Seigneur, notre ami, notre camarade
Toi qui écartas du visage de la prostituée
Comme un rideau de roseaux ses longs cheveux
Sur la source de ses larmes[58]

So like a burning coal
So like a burning coal in a white rose bush
the gold buckler of their fortunes
They whitened His Black Face with the spit of their
cold contempt

They spat on Your Black Face,
Our Lord, our friend, our comrade
You who pushed from the whore's face
The long hair that lay over the source of her tears
Like a reed curtain

The first stanza references two colors: Black represented by the word *"charbon"* "coal" and white. The anaphora in the first two lines amplifies the comparison made by the poet. The word *"charbon"* is tied to transformation by heat. By changing the color of Jesus, who represents the source of their fortune, they can use his image as they please while denying or concealing what he is supposed to represent. We also notice that the color Black is directly tied to Jesus' face: *"Sa Face noire"* "his Black face." The second stanza describes in depth the relationship between the narrator and Jesus. The expression *"Ils ont craché sur Ta Face noire"* "They spat on Your Black face" is revealing. First, the possessive adjective "Ta" "your" shows the proximity, friendship that exists between the narrator and Jesus. Second, the poet uses the adjective *"Noire"* "Black" to describe Jesus' face again. The possessive adjective *"notre"* "our" insinuates that Jesus is not only the narrator's *"ami"* "friend" and *"camarade"* "comrade," but he is also the friend and comrade of the group of people to which the narrator belongs. The last two lines refer to a Biblical story in which Jesus cast out multiple demons from a disenfranchised person called Mary Magdalene. Once healed from the evil spirits, she decided to become one of Jesus' followers. The phrase *"la source de ses larmes"* "the source of her tears" references the evil spirits that Jesus removed that had previously possessed her. By mentioning this episode, the poet calls to mind the compassion of Jesus toward the troubled, neglected, or rejected people in society. The possessive adjective *"notre"* "our" serves to contrast the relation between Christ and whites with the relation of Christ and Blacks, two relationships that Roumain has already contextualized for the reader. He describes the oppressors:

> *Ils ont fait*
> *les riches les pharisiens les propriétaires fonciers*
> *les banquiers*
> *Ils ont fait de l'Homme saignant le dieu sanglant*
> *Oh Judas ricane*
> *Oh judas ricane:*
> *Christ entre deux voleurs comme une flamme déchirée*
> *au sommet du monde*
> *Allumait la révolte des esclaves*[59]

> They made
> the rich, the hypocrites, the landowners,
> the bankers
>
> They made the bleeding man into the bloody god
> Oh Judas sneers
> Oh Judas sneers:
> Christ between two thieves like a flame torn asunder
> at the top of the world
> Lit up the revolt of the slaves

Roumain's mention of usurious bankers as a vital component of the oppression of the poor reinforces the powerlessness of people to find a way out of their misery. Roumain recalls his previous statement about those in power and their efforts to take advantage of others' suffering to ensure their own privilege. These verses imply that the rich and the landowners in their quest for wealth and power in Haiti tried to maximize profits while neglecting human dignity and the authentic word of the Lord. Bankers, who are theoretically supposed to offer loans to people with financial difficulties, only made them available to wealthy people. The small amount of funding that is available to the poor is given at an interest rate so high that it is not an exaggeration to assume that it keeps poor people in bondage.[60] The hypocrites are those who pretend to be Christians, but whose actions betray the genuine gospel of Christ. They are compared to Judas; they betray Christ, as they have betrayed the Blacks, for their own profit: Roumain depicts this ideological and theological burglary in the following manner, *"Mais Christ aujourd'hui est dans la main des voleurs"*[61] "But Christ today is in the house of thieves." Christ's true nature has been so abused that little remains of the sermons of the bleeding man. In this way, the new sermon is not entirely new, but revives the true Christ that has been lost within institutional Christianity. The *"Nouveau Sermon Nègre"* is not only a rebellion against the longstanding oppressive gospel, but also a return to Christ's teaching of humanity. It portrays the attempts of those who follow the timeworn sermon to profit from the dehumanization form of Christ, from his betrayal:

> *Mais Christ aujourd'hui est dans la maison des voleurs*
> *Et ses bras déploient dans les cathédrales l'ombre étendue*
> *du vautour*
> *Et dans les caves des monastères le prêtre compte les*
> *intérêts des trente deniers*
> *Et les clochers des églises crachent la mort sur les*
> *multitudes affamées*[62]

> But Christ today is in the house of thieves
> And his arms spread out in the cathedrals are the extended
> shadow of the vulture
> And in the caves of the monasteries the priest counts the
> interest on thirty pieces of silver
> And the bell towers of the Churches spit Death on the
> hungry multitudes

These lines carry great importance. Full of images, they reveal the true meanings of the Catholic Church symbols. First, the picture of Jesus with his arms wide open in the cathedrals, which should signify a welcome environment, is associated with scavengers, known for eating carcasses of dead animals. They devour without mercy. Second, "Les trente deniers" "thirty pieces of silver" refer to the money that Judas Iscariot received for betraying Jesus, thus helping the Roman soldiers identify him during his arrest. Referencing the priest inside the monastery as the one counting the interest of such money, the narrator points out the complicity of the Church in betraying the teaching of Jesus and portrays the Church as an untrustworthy institution. Moreover, the bell, which is used both to remind people of the time of the day and to call them to Church services, serves as an instrument to invite Church members to Church in order to bring their large offerings which contribute to their impoverishment and misery. It also implies that Churches do too little to alleviate poverty among their members. Roumain sympathizes with the debased and dehumanized Christ. Moreover, Roumain underscores that the Church is part of the problem, because its leaders are not true to Christ's teachings. Roumain points out the humanity of Christ, his teaching, his modest life among ordinary people and his compassion toward them. Yet, the rich and the powerful manipulate his image and use it to their advantage. In that sense the defender of the poor becomes the accomplices of thieves. It is in that context that Franck Laraque mentions: "*Au nom de ce Dieu contrefait, de puissants leaders politiques appuyés par des chefs religieux, se confèrent la mission "civilisatrice" de conquérir par le feu et par les armes, causant terreur et panique.*" (Franck Laraque 155) "In the name of this counterfeit God, powerful political leaders supported by religious leaders, take on the "civilizing" mission of conquering by fire and arms, causing terror and panic."

Roumain ends "*Nouveau Sermon Nègre*" with a call to arms. He wants to retrieve Christ and empower those who fought against their oppressors. For this reason:

Nous ne leur pardonnerons pas car ils savent ce
Qu'ils font
Ils ont lynché John qui organisait le syndicat
Ils l'ont chassé comme un loup hagard avec des chiens
à travers bois
Ils l'ont pendu en riant au tronc du vieux sycomore[63]

We will not forgive them for they know
what they do
They lynched John who worked to organize the people
They chased him through the woods with dogs
Like a gaunt wolf
Laughing they hung him to the trunk of the old sycamore

Unlike Jesus who asked God to forgive his killers and enemies, the poet offers no forgiveness to people who purposely mistreat others because "*Il [Roumain] pense qu'il est illogique de répondre aux offenses, aux injustices et à l'exploitation par le pardon.*"[64] (Toussaint 109) "He [Roumain] thinks that it is illogical to respond to offenses, injustices and exploitation with forgiveness." The reference to John lends itself to a dual implication. The biblical tone of the poem would lead the reader to recall John the Baptist, who was executed because others feared that he would start a rebellion. Yet another rebellious John faced such a fate: John Brown (1800–1859), who led the failed raid of the Federal Armory at Harpers Ferry, West Virginia in 1859, was hanged. Unlike John the Baptist, John Brown was lynched. The reference to the revered abolitionist is also worthy of note. An additional mocking of life occurs in the line in which they, "*en riant*"[65] "laughing" use a sycamore tree, the biblical tree of life, to hang John. Roumain's imagery challenges the notion of Christ taking an active role in forgiving violence against him because those who carried it out are ignorant. In fact, Roumain actually implies that the ferocity of the aggression against Christ (i.e., the Black people), was calculated and deliberate. Moreover, killing John was designed to inculcate terror and discourage any ideas of a slave revolt.

CHAPTER 3

Therefore, Roumain calls for Blacks to abandon passivity:

Non, frères, camarades
Nous ne prierons plus
Notre révolte s'élève comme le cri de l'oiseau de tempête
au-dessus du clapotement pourri des marécages
Nous ne chanterons plus les tristes spirituals désespérés
Un autre chant jaillit de nos gorges[66]

No, brothers, comrades
We will pray no more
Our revolt is rising like the cry of a bird of the storm
above the rotten sloshing of the swamp
We will no longer sing the sad hopeless spirituals
Another song rises from our throats

The negative word "*non*" "no" coupled with the negative future tense expresses the desire of the narrator to follow a different path. "*Nous ne prierons plus*" "we will pray no more" relays the idea that, from that point on, things would be different. The words "*révolte*" "revolt," "*s'élève*" "is rising," "*cri*" "cry," *tempête* "storm," and "*au-dessus*" "above" suggest an escalation, a disturbance, or a different way of stirring up the peace that one cannot ignore. The poet clearly expresses the will and desire for an uprising like this to happen. While Coulthard argues that, "The poem ends with a complete rejection of Christianity,"[67] (239) an alternative examination of the text, which I propose, shows that Roumain doesn't urge his contemporaries to abandon the Christian faith altogether; he merely urges Black people to be aware of the maneuvering of some Church leaders in order to maintain the status quo. He laid the foundations of Black liberation theology. Through these verses, he advises his colleagues to participate actively in their liberation. As he saw it, prayer is an essential part of a religion; however, it is only a tool to be used in conjunction with actions. Roumain felt that there was value in prayer, however, after praying, one must act. By promoting such an idea, he preaches against the gospel of resignation. He fights against passive Christians who believe that it is enough merely to call on God for help without doing anything to improve their situation. Roumain encourages people to take action. Instead of kneeling while awaiting a miracle, he invites them to bear arms to defend their cause. Therefore, he proposes a new song of life by claiming that while God is there to help people, they must also use the resources at their disposal to improve their situation:

Nous déployons nos rouges drapeaux
Tachés du sang de nos justes
Sous ce signe nous marcherons
Sous ce signe nous marchons

Debout les damnés de la terre
Debout les forçats de la faim[68]

We unfurl our red flags
Stained with the blood of our people
Under this symbol we will march
Under this symbol we march
Rise up damned of the earth
Rise up prisoners of starvation

The phrase *"Nous déployons nos rouges drapeaux"* "We unfurl our red flags" expresses a sense of pride. Red is the color of communism. The phrase is delivered at a point at which the narrator and his comrades are no longer afraid of showing their teeth and their capabilities. The anaphora, *"sous ce signe"* "under this symbol" further amplifies this sentiment. Strength and unity are portrayed in the repetition of the last four lines and in the military language of *"nous marcherons"* "we will march," *"marchons"* "we march" and *"debout"* "rise up." The poet emphasized that the neglected will stand tall, and he announces a new world, pure and hallowed, which will replace the tainted world of injustice. One can infer that this new world is devoid of foreign occupation. The new sermon serves as a call for Blacks to rise against not only their oppressors, but also against those who oppressed the rightful word of Christ. The analogy of the Black struggle and Christ gives the poem divine justification. In remarking on *"Nouveau Sermon Nègre,"* Jean wrote:

> *Le Nègre ne bercera plus sa souffrance par des "spiritual désespérés"; l'heure est à la violence, la violence révolutionnaire qui détruit le masque jusque dans sa racine. Le Nègre récuse maintenant le pacifisme de l'Église, en faisant Chorus avec la bourgeoisie et le pouvoir, a trahi Jésus, l'ami et le défenseur des humbles. Le Nègre repousse cet opium de la résignation que lui verse une religion vénale, hypocrite, à la solde des exploiteurs. Il passe à la révolte, une révolte sanglante qui applique la loi du Talion.*[69] (24)

The Negro will no longer cradle his suffering with "desperate spirituals"; the time has come for violence, revolutionary violence that destroys the mask at its roots. The Negro now rejects the pacifism of the Church, which, by making chorus with the bourgeoisie and the power, has betrayed Jesus, the friend and defender of the humble. The Negro rejects this opium of resignation that a venal, hypocritical religion, in the pay of the exploiters, pours into him. He turns to revolt, a bloody revolt that applies the law of Talion.

In the poem, Roumain parallels the defamation of Blacks under white rule with the defamation of Christ by a powerful and ill-advised Church. He shows how Western institutional powers sought to twist and manipulate both Blacks and Christ to serve themselves, and he maintains that Western powers have become so egregious that they no longer respect the teachings and sacraments of God himself. He implies that the former colonizers and oppressors of the Western world achieved their avaricious and ruthless goals of acquiring wealth and power by abusing others under the guise of spreading Christianity:

> In the "New Negro Sermon," Roumain declares his righteous postcolonial wage against the oppressors of Black people and the oppressors of the oppressed of the world after he denounces the institutional Church—the tool of Western colonization—and the great white crime of slavery, white supremacy, and western colonization facilitated through the Christian *mission civilisatrice*."[70] (Joseph 70–71)

Thus, Roumain accuses those in power of vitiating Christianity and its teachings because they do not practice the principles on which Christianity was founded. In this way, the Church in Roumain's poem is not a holy institution, but one that robs and steals without regard for the poor. It can be said that Roumain accuses the Church of appropriating Christ, and Roumain is proposing reclaiming him, albeit in a distinctive way. Therefore, a new sermon that is not only endogenous, but also in line with the true virtues of Christ, is needed. The notion of marching under "*nos drapeaux*" "our flags" depicts Roumain's belief in the populist solution to Western ethnocentrism that ignored African culture and its people. In the last two stanzas, the true anger of the people is expressed and immortalized with revolutionary tones, as Roumain advocates abandoning passive behavior and uniting the oppressed people across the world to take back the dignity of which they were historically deprived for so long.

Many critics agree on the dimension of Jacques Roumain's works. For example, Trouillot (137)[71], Thadal (37)[72], and Laraque (153)[73] agree that Roumain's work goes beyond the agenda of the Negritude movement to embrace the plight of all the neglected and disenfranchised all over the world. Leconte sees Roumain's poetry as: *"un immense cri du cœur qui appelle Haïti aux armes et qui invite tous les damnés de la terre et les forçats de la faim à se mettre debout et à renverser les citadelles qui les emprisonnent partout dans un monde coercitif et invivable."*[74] (210) "an immense cry from the heart that calls Haiti to arms and invites all the damned of the earth and the forçats of hunger to stand up and overthrow the citadels that imprison them everywhere in a coercive and unbearable world."

Conclusion

Jacques Roumain's contribution to the Development of the identity of the Haitian nation and its self-determination cannot be overstated. Neither can the depth and the consistency of his commitment to fight, via literary means and organizing and participating in social protests throughout his lifetime, against Haitian society's deeply contested spaces. While the American occupation sought to perpetuate poverty through the imposition of taxes, Roumain was shaping an intellectual and social resistance to take back a Haiti that he envisioned as possible. It is well known that the occupiers killed thousands of Haitian patriots, reinstated the *corvée*, appropriated much land from peasants and otherwise spared no effort in establishing systems favorable to themselves and the privileged. It is also accurate to state that there were Haitian intellectuals who opposed the occupiers. However, other Haitian intellectuals were unwilling to follow in Roumain's footsteps since he suffered greatly by enduring multiple beatings, torture and incarcerations when he could have had an infinitely more comfortable and less endangered life. Although Roumain was a perspicacious critic of the Haitian Catholic Church and its role of collusion with the American occupancy, he stated unequivocally, "*Je respecte la religion, toutes les religions.*" (*OEuvres complètes*, 787) "I respect religion, all religions." He understood Christ as a fellow champion of the poor, and he also stood firmly against the Haitian Catholic Church's campaign and criminalization of Voodoo. Jacques Roumain defended the concept that religion should be used as an instrument to change people's material condition as well as their spiritual need. His willingness to take the road less traveled and reaffirm that decision has forever changed the literary and social legacies of the country that he valued so categorically. The American brutality toward Haitian peasants is reminiscent of slavery, and Roumain made sure that uniform normalization of terror and brutality would not go unchallenged. Thanks to the elegance of his writing and the extensiveness of his attacks against all forms of social injustice, his literary and social legacies will continue to exert their power even though nearly two Roumain lifetimes have elapsed since his.

Notes

1. Dash, J. Michael. "Introduction." *Masters of the Dew*. Translated by Langston Hughes and Mercer Cook. Portsmouth: Heinemann Educational Books, 1978.
2. For more information on this matter see Hogar Nicolas (*L'Occupation américaine d'Haïti : La revanche de l'histoire*. Madrid: Industrias Gráficas España, 1955); Hans Schmidt (*The United States Occupation of Haiti*. USA: Rutgers University Press, 1971).
3. Gaillard, Roger. *L'univers romanesque de Jacques Roumain*. Port-au-Prince : Henri Deschamps, 1975.
4. Dorsinville, Roger. *Jacques Roumain*. Paris : Présence Africaine, 1981.
5. Jean, Eddy Arnold. *L'immense Cri des damnés de la terre : Études sur Jacques Roumain, Jean F. Brière, Rousan Camille, Jacques S. Alexis*. Port-au-Prince: Courrier d'Haïti, 1975.
6. Carolyn Fowler wrote the first biography on Roumain and provides insightful commentaries on Roumain's interaction with religion.
   Fowler, Carolyn. *A Knot in the Thread: The Life and Work of Jacques Roumain*. Washington: D.C Howard University Press, 1980.

[7] *La Revue Indigène* published six issues between July 1927 and February 1928.
[8] Nzengou-Tayo, Marie-José. "Creole and French in Haitian Literature" in *The Haitian Creole Language: History, Structure, Use, and Education*. United States: Lexington Books, 2010.
[9] Jean-Claude Michel quotes Depestre who, in his book called *"Pour la Révolution," Pour la Poésie* mentions that: "Well before the publication of *Légitime Défense* in 1932, Roumain was among the redactors of the first Black review being published in Paris: *Le Cri des Nègres* (Negro Voices) (131)".

Michel, Jean-Claude. *The Black Surrealists*. New York: Peter Lang Publishing, 2000.
Depestre, René. *Pour la révolution, pour la poésie*. Leméac, 1974.

[10] Thadal, Marc Roland. *Jacques Roumain : L'unité d'une œuvre*. Port-au-Prince : Editions des Antilles, 1997.
[11] *"Le texte de Roumain, au-delà de sa réussite littéraire, transcende la neutralité sécurisante pour se muer en écriture de témoignage, de combat, de contestation et de condamnation des dérives et catastrophes d'une société pourtant organizable."*

Leconte, Frantz-Antoine. *Jacques Roumain et Haïti : La mission du poète dans la cité*. Paris: L'Harmattan, 2011.

[12] *"Il a connu deux fois la prison, et de multiples organisations de jeunes lui doivent alors leur validité. Il est déjà un 'leader'."*

Gaillard, Roger. *L'univers romanesque de Jacques Roumain*. Port-au-Prince : Henri Deschamps, 1975.

[13] A report called "A Review of the Finances of the Republic of Haiti (1924–1930)" was submitted to the American High Commission by S. DE LA RUE, the Financial Adviser-General Receiver in March 1930. <https://ufdc.ufl.edu/AA00001155/00001/3>
[14] Roumain, Jacques. *Œuvres complètes*. Paris : Collection Archivos, 2003.
[15] Toussaint, Hérold. *L'utopie révolutionnaire en Haïti : Autour de Jacques Roumain*. Port-au-Prince : Presses Nationales d'Haïti, 2012.
[16] *"Le vrai motif de l'intervention américaine dans ces régions [en Amérique] est que les Etats-Unis, ayant atteint le stade impérialiste de leur développement économique, cherchent à assurer à leurs capitaux et à leurs investissements le maximum de garantie et de profit."*

Makouta-Mboukou, Jean-Pierre. *Jacques Roumain : Essai sur la signification spirituelle et religieuse de son œuvre*. Dissertation. L'Université de Paris IV. February 8, 1975.

[17] Cobb, Martha. *Harlem, Haiti and Havana: A comparative Critical Study of Langston Hughes, Jacques Roumain, Nicolás Guillén*. Washington D.C: Three Continent Press, 1979.
[18] *"… il recevait des tracts de l'étranger. On l'accusa d'en recevoir des armes, de détenir même un plan du Palais national devant faciliter l'assassinat du Président. Il fut déféré à une Cour martiale, jugé, condamné."*

Dorsinville, Roger. *Jacques Roumain*. Paris: Présence Africaine, 1981.

[19] *"En 1929, Roumain fut jeté en prison pour avoir dirigé les grèves estudiantines, et mis le feu à l'actuel Ciné-Paramount… Relâché, il fut incarcéré une nouvelle fois à cause de ses articles virulents contre le gouvernement et ses laquais. Il fut condamné cette fois à trois ans de prison."*

Jean, Eddy Arnold. *L'immense Cri des damnés de la terre : Études sur Jacques Roumain, Jean F. Brière, Rousan Camille, Jacques S. Alexis*. Port-au-Prince: Courrier d'Haïti, 1975.

[20] La *corvée* is an old law according to which peasants in Haiti had to work six days a year to repair or maintain roads in the areas where they lived. In order to build roads, the Americans

reinstated la *corvée* and ordered the peasants to work not only outside their district, but well beyond the time set by the law.

21 "La même année, Roumain fut arrêté par le gouvernement démagogue de Vincent et condamné à deux ans de prison. Sa peine expurgée, Roumain dut s'exiler."
   Jean, Eddy Arnold. *L'immense Cri des damnés de la terre : Études sur Jacques Roumain, Jean F. Brière, Rousan Camille, Jacques S. Alexis*. Port-au-Prince: Courrier d'Haïti, 1975.

22 In writing about Roumain's exile in Europe, Michael Dash mentions that: "Politically, he was among those writers who tried to arouse the world's conscience over the tragedy of the Spanish Civil War. The poem Madrid, written at that time, reveals his idealism and the conception of an international fraternity struggling against Fascist domination." (*Introduction*, 7)

23 Trouillot, Hénock. *Dimension et limites de Jacques Roumain*. Port-au-Prince : Édition Fardin, 1975.

24 Roumain, Jacques. "La Poésie comme arme." *Cahiers D'Haïti*, II, no.4 (1944) pp 37–40.

25 Leconte, Frantz-Antoine. *Jacques Roumain et Haïti : La mission du poète dans la cité*. Paris: L'Harmattan, 2011. It is worth mentioning that the Catholic Church fought superstition everywhere, including Europe and Asia. It defined superstition as the act of diverting or corrupting the worship that ought to be devoted to God (the Creator) for the benefit of the creature.

26 Toussaint, Hérold. *L'utopie révolutionnaire en Haïti : Autour de Jacques Roumain*. Port-au-Prince : Presses Nationales d'Haïti, 2012.

27 Ibid., 115.

28 Makouta-Mboukou, Jean-Pierre. *Jacques Roumain : Essai sur la signification spirituelle et religieuse de son œuvre*. Dissertation. L'Université de Paris IV. February 8, 1975.

29 "Loa are the Voodoo spirits called upon by practitioners in order to make a request, whether it's to improve one's romantic life or heal a loved one's sickness. Since each loa is responsible for a different aspect of life, there are hundreds of these spirits, and each has their own veve symbol used to invoke them." <https://www.ranker.com/list/facts-about-loa-Voodoo-spirits/erin-mccann>

30 Joseph, Celucien L. *Thinking in Public: Faith, Secular Humanism, and Development in Jacques Roumain*. Eugene: PICKWICK Publications, 2017.

31 Ibid., 248–249.

32 Ibid., 251.

33 Joseph, Celucien L. *Thinking in Public: Faith, Secular Humanism, and Development in Jacques Roumain*. Eugene: PICKWICK Publications, 2017.

34 Voodoo Priest.

35 Ceremony for a Voodoo spirit.

36 During the American occupation of Haiti, France and the United States reached the understanding that the Americans would make French the official language of Haiti, allow the French Catholic Church to continue its evangelical work in Haiti peacefully, and let France maintain control of the Haitian school system.

37 "Pour reprocher à la plupart des membres du clergé leur mépris de la culture haïtienne, pour préciser le lien entre le vaudou et les conditions socioéconomiques en Haïti, pour prôner des transformations sociales et économiques en Haïti"
   Toussaint, Hérold. *L'utopie révolutionnaire en Haïti : Autour de Jacques Roumain*. Port-au-Prince : Presses Nationales d'Haïti, 2012.

38. Joseph, Celucien L. *Thinking in Public: Faith, Secular Humanism, and Development in Jacques Roumain*. Eugene: PICKWICK Publications, 2017.
39. Jacques Roumain. *À propos de la campagne "anti-supersticieuse."* Port-au-Prince : Imprimerie de l'État, 1942.
40. Joseph, Celucien L. *Thinking in Public: Faith, Secular Humanism, and Development in Jacques Roumain*. Eugene: PICKWICK Publications, 2017.
41. Ibid., 252.
42. Ibid., 258.
43. Some of Roumain's better known papers are "Contribution à l'étude de l'ethnobotanique précolombienne des Grandes Antilles," *Bulletin du Bureau d'Ethnologie de la République d'Haïti* (BERH), février 1942 ; "Le sacrifice du tambour Assôtô(r)," *Bulletin du* BERH, mars 1943 ; "L'outillage lithique des Ciboney d'Haïti," *Bulletin du* BERH, 1943.
44. "In 1943 President Élie Lescot appointed Roumain chargé d'affaires at the Haitian embassy in Mexico. This job was accepted because of a directive from the Communist Party which thought it was strategic to have famous Marxists placed in important public positions. It was a difficult decision for Roumain as he ran the risk of appearing to compromise himself politically" (Dash, *Introduction*, 9).
45. Jernegan, Marcus W. "Slavery and Conversion in the American Colonies," *The American Historical Review* 21: 3 (1916).
46. Fanon, Frantz, *The Wretched of the Earth*. New York: Grove Press, 2004.
47. Coulthard, G. R. "Rejection of European Culture as a Theme in Caribbean Literature," *Caribbean Quarterly*, 5: 4 (1959): 239.
48. For example, see the poem "I don't like Africa" by Paul Niger (Guadeloupe) published in Léopold Sédar Senghor's *La Nouvelle Poésie Nègre et* Malgache (1948) and the book entitled A New Song (1945) by the Haitian writer René Piqion.
49. Kennedy, Ellen Conroy. *The Negritude poets: An Anthology of Translations from the French*. New York: Thunder's Mouth Press, 1989.
50. Jacques Roumain, *Ebony wood. Bois-d'ébène. Poems*. The French text with a translation by Sidney Shapiro. Interworld Press, 1972, 26.
51. Roumain, *Ebony wood*, 26.
52. Roumain, *Ebony wood*, 26.
53. During slavery, the colonizers used the Bible as an instrument to enslave indigenous people and make them obedient.
54. Roumain, *Ebony wood*, 26.
55. Ibid., 26.
56. Ibid., 26.
57. Ibid., 26.
58. Ibid., 27.
59. Roumain, *Ebony wood*, 28.
60. Lundahl, Mats. *Peasants and Poverty: A Study of Haiti*, Croom Helm, 1979.
61. Roumain, *Ebony wood*, 28.
62. Ibid., 28.
63. Ibid., 28.
64. Toussaint, Hérold. *L'utopie révolutionnaire en Haïti : Autour de Jacques Roumain*. Port-au-Prince : Presses Nationales d'Haïti, 2012.

65 Roumain, *Ebony wood*, 28.
66 Ibid., 29.
67 Coulthard, G. R. "Rejection of European Culture as a Theme in Caribbean Literature," *Caribbean Quarterly*, 5: 4 (1959): 239.
68 Roumain, *Ebony wood*, 30.
69 Jean, Eddy Arnold. *L'immense Cri des damnés de la terre : Études sur Jacques Roumain, Jean F. Brière, Rousan Camille, Jacques S. Alexis*. Port-au-Prince : Courrier d'Haïti, 1975.
70 Joseph, Celucien L. *Thinking in Public: Faith, Secular Humanism, and Development in Jacques Roumain*. Eugene: PICKWICK Publications, 2017.
71 Trouillot, Hénock. *Dimension et limites de Jacques Roumain*. Port-au-Prince : Edition Fardin, 1975.
72 Thadal, Marc Roland. *Jacques Roumain : L'unité d'une œuvre*. Port-au-Prince : Editions des Antilles, 1997.
73 Laraque, Franck. "Fulgurante de l'image dans la poésie révolutionnaire de Jacques Roumain." *Jacques Roumain et Haïti : La mission du poète dans la cité*. Paris : L'Harmattan, 2011.
74 Leconte, Frantz-Antoine. *Jacques Roumain et Haïti : La mission du poète dans la cité*. Paris: L'Harmattan, 2011.

Bibliography

Cobb, Martha. *Harlem, Haiti and Havana: A comparative Critical Study of Langston Hughes, Jacques Roumain, Nicolás Guillén*. Washington D.C: Three Continent Press, 1979.

Clorméus, Lewis A. « Des leaders protestants haïtiens dans la vague anticléricale et nationaliste (1927–1929) ». The Journal of Haitian Studies, vol. 21, no 2, 2015, p. 88–120.

———. *Entre l'État, les élites et les religions en Haïti : redécouvrir la campagne anti-superstitieuse de 1939–1942*. Thèse de doctorat, EHESS/ UEH, 2012.

Coulthard, G. R. "Rejection of European Culture as a Theme in Caribbean Literature," *Caribbean Quarterly*, 5: 4 (1959): 239.

Dash, J. Michael. "Introduction." *Masters of the Dew*. Translated by Langston Hughes and Mercer Cook. Portsmouth: Heinemann Educational Books, 1978.

Depestre, René. "Liminaire : parler de Jacques Roumain." Jacques Roumain : Œuvres *complètes*. Paris : Collections Archivos, 2003.

———. *Pour la révolution, pour la poésie*. Leméac, 1974.

Dorsinville, Roger. *Jacques Roumain*. Paris: Présence Africaine, 1981.

Fanon, Frantz, *The Wretched of the Earth*. New York: Grove Press, 2004.

Fowler, Carolyn. *A Knot in the Thread: The Life and Work of Jacques Roumain*. Washington : D.C Howard University Press, 1980.

Gaillard, Roger. *L'univers romanesque de Jacques Roumain*. Port-au-Prince : Henri Deschamps, 1975.

Jean, Eddy Arnold. *L'immense Cri des damnés de la terre : Études sur Jacques Roumain, Jean F. Brière, Rousan Camille, Jacques S. Alexis*. Port-au-Prince : Courrier d'Haïti, 1975.

Jernegan, Marcus W. "Slavery and Conversion in the American Colonies," *The American Historical Review* 21: 3 (1916).

Joseph, Celucien L. *Thinking in Public: Faith, Secular Humanism, and Development in Jacques Roumain*. Eugene: PICKWICK Publications, 2017.

Kennedy, Ellen Conroy. *The Negritude poets: An Anthology of Translations from the French*. New York: Thunder's Mouth Press, 1989.

Laraque, Franck. "Fulgurante de l'image dans la poésie révolutionnaire de Jacques Roumain." *Jacques Roumain et Haïti : La mission du poète dans la cité*. Paris : L'Harmattan, 2011.

Leconte, Frantz-Antoine. *Jacques Roumain et Haïti : La mission du poète dans la cité*. Paris: L'Harmattan, 2011.

Mats Lundahl, *Peasants and Poverty: A Study of Haiti*. London : Croom Helm, 1979.

Makouta-Mboukou, Jean-Pierre. Jacques Roumain : *Essai sur la signification spirituelle et religieuse de son œuvre*. Dissertation. L'Université de Paris IV. February 8, 1975.

Michel, Jean-Claude. *The Black Surrealists*. New York: Peter Lang Publishing, 2000.

Nicolas, Hogar. *L'Occupation américaine d'Haïti : La revanche de l'histoire*. Madrid: Industrias Gráficas España, 1955

Nzengou-Tayo, Marie-José. "Creole and French in Haitian Literature" in *The Haitian Creole Language: History, Structure, Use, and Education*. United States: Lexington Books, 2010.

Robertshaw, Matthew. "Occupying Creole: The Crisis of Language under the US Occupation of Haiti." *The Journal of Haitian Studies*, Volume 24, No. 1, 2018.

Roumain, Jacques. *À propos de la campagne "anti-supersticieuse."* Port-au-Prince : Imprimerie de l'État, 1942.

———. *Ebony wood. Bois-d'ébène. Poems*. The French text with a translation by Sidney Shapiro. New York: Interworld Press, 1972.

———. "La Poésie comme arme." *Cahiers D'Haïti*, II, no.4 (1944) pp. 37–40.

———. *Œuvres complètes*. Paris: Collection Archivos, 2003.

Schmidt, Hans. *The United States Occupation of Haiti*. USA: Rutgers University Press, 1971.

Souffrant, Claude. *Une Négritude socialiste : religion et développement chez J. Roumain, J. et L. Hugues.* Paris: L'Harmattan, 1978.

Thadal, Marc Roland. *Jacques Roumain : L'unité d'une œuvre.* Port-au-Prince : Editions des Antilles, 1997.

Toussaint, Hérold. *L'utopie révolutionnaire en Haïti : Autour de Jacques Roumain.* Port-au-Prince : Presses Nationales d'Haïti, 2012.

Trouillot, Hénock. *Dimension et limites de Jacques Roumain.* Port-au-Prince : Edition Fardin, 1975.

CHAPTER 4

The Representation of Women's Incarceration During the Duvalier Regimes: Anne-Christine d'Adesky's Feminist Perspective in *Under the Bone*

Introduction

Anne-Christine d'Adesky (1958–X) is a polyglot American AIDS advocate, author, journalist, and documentarian filmmaker. She wrote for *New York Native*, OUT, *The Nation*, *The Village Voice*, the *Washington Post*, *The Nation*, and *Los Angeles Times*. Through her work, she aims to fight poverty, advocate for social justice, and provide the disenfranchised an opportunity to express their concerns. She contributed extensively to the fight against the HIV/AIDS epidemics, and in 2005, she co-produced a documentary film called, "Pills, Profit, Protest: Chronicle of the Global AIDS Movement," that was broadcast on the ShowTime cable television channel in the United States. Her first novel, *Under the Bone*, which will be analyzed in this chapter, was published in 1994.

Some of the themes that run through the entirety of *Under the Bone* such as social and economic inequality, gender inequality and political corruption continue to be present in works that she produced subsequently. Her second book, *Moving Mountains: The Race to Treat Global AIDS*, was published in 2004. It is a book in which d'Adesky documents the difficulties as well as some of the successful efforts made internationally in order to provide treatment for AIDS patients. Her detailed field work offers sound data that analyzes the AIDS crisis in nine countries: Brazil, Cuba, Haiti, India, Mexico, Morocco, Russia, South Africa, and Uganda. D'Adesky provides statistics about the ravages of AIDS and laments the lack of services in rural areas around the world. Her observation leads her to conclude that:

> It is possible to treat the poorest people effectively with AIDS drugs, and it costs less to do than [was] projected. The barrier to access is not poverty, or illiteracy, or the inability of Africans to take their drugs consistently, or other indices of national Development

CHAPTER 4

or capacity; it is a lack of political commitment pure and simple. (d'Adesky, *Moving Mountains*, 319)

The book was well-received by critics. For example, the scholar Sue Holden argues that: "D'Adesky shows how treatment gaps between rich and poor countries are not historically given but are instead actively created and reproduced by powerful individuals and groups in business and in politics."[1] (Holden, 127). In that "well-researched book"[2] (McGough, 617), d'Adesky points out the attention that the AIDS crisis has gained intentionally, the progress that has been made "and describes the major obstacles to treatment."[3] (McGough, p. 617) In her work, she does not just observe and report. According to the scholar Karen Kahn, "d'Adesky pushes her readers to embrace their responsibility for this human tragedy and join the struggle to make treatment accessible around the world."[4] (p. 24)

Her third book, *Beyond Shock: Charting the Landscape of Sexual Violence in post-Quake Haiti* was published in 2014. The scholar Claudine Michel, editor of Journal of Haitian Studies, summarizes the book in the following quote:

> *Beyond Shock* offers the first comprehensive examination of sexual violence in the aftermath of Haiti's January 2010 earthquake. Journalist Anne-Christine d'Adesky weaves together findings by more than 60 sources, reporting the struggle by victims to rebuild their lives and documenting the progress made by frontline providers of services to these survivors.[5]

Her most recent oeuvre, *The Pox Lover: An Activist's Decade in New York and Paris*, published in 2017 was a finalist for the 2018 Lambda Literary Award in the category of Lesbian Memoir and Biography. The book is a personal account by d'Adesky about many events that took place in the 1990s in both Paris and New York. It highlights d'Adesky's long history of activism in the areas of civic and social justice. In particular, it shows her involvement in AIDS and ACT UP through multiple protests. For example, d'Adesky tells the story of her activism against Cardinal John O'Connor who opposed the distribution of condoms, and talks about prevention and safe sex. One day, she went to a mass presided by the priest, and she challenged him on those issues while he was preaching. Many people were shocked, and she was escorted out and arrested. At a time when the medication for AIDS victims was not effective, many people that she knew personally lost their lives in New York as well as in Paris. Since she suffered from insomnia, she spent countless nights observing people's movements and activities. She observed that among the activists that she was documenting, there were many friendships, affairs, break-ups, and addictions. Through it all, humor and music were of great help to the group of activists. Art was used as a way to express their activism, find ways to treat the disease, and provide access to treatment. She mentions Paris as a city to which she went for both work and romance. Her nightly walks along the Seine, the great river, were enjoyable. In Paris, she also witnessed the harsh rhetoric of Jean-Marie Le Pen, the founder of the right-wing populist party called Le Front National. She describes him as a xenophobe who was very vocal against ACT UP. She also observed how both Paris and New York changed through gentrification. This book also touches on her family heritage. As the critic Sarah Schulman points out: "D'Adesky's memoir also reveals her family's role in French colonialism, raising compelling questions about privilege, survival, homophobia, and dislocation."[6] She was the recipient of the first Award of Courage from amfAR, the Foundation for AIDS Research.

This chapter addresses some crucial questions about how d'Adesky inscribes the incarceration of women, as well as the methods she uses to reveal details regarding that experience in her first novel, *Under the Bone*. I argue that by utilizing an eclectic narrative approach to demonstrate the plight of Haitian women, d'Adesky tackles the theme of imprisonment to unearth the atrocity and injustice Haitian women faced during the Duvalier dictatorship. Her fictionalized account includes stories, memos, letters, interior monologues, medical and legal documents, and taken together, they offer a plausible fictional account of how Haitian women have actively contributed to the struggle against political oppression.

Biography of Anne-Christine d'Adesky

Anne-Christine d'Adesky was born in Marquette, Michigan in 1958. Her father was born in Port-au-Prince, Haiti, and her mother was born in Grenoble, France. In my interview with her, on October 6, 2023, d'Adesky confirmed that she grew up in a Francophone family:

> In fact, we were not allowed to speak English in our family. Every time we said an English word, they [her parents] wanted us to put a penny in a jar. So, my parents got rich. I think I was very much affected and framed by my parents' values, which were both reflecting the colonizers and the colonized, as I think of them.[7]

She was required to learn French, but her father did not want her to learn Creole. Nonetheless, her parents used to take her and her siblings to Haiti and to France in order to be familiar with both countries and cultures. As d'Adesky pointed out: "We would be taken to Haiti for the summer vacation to study French in the heat of the day. And then in August, we would then get taken to the other set of grandparents who were in France."[8]

According to her testimony, when she was growing up in Haiti, d'Adesky was very uncomfortable from a very young age with respect to the privilege that her

CHAPTER 4

family had. It was obvious to her that this inequity was highly discriminatory. That is why when she was approximately 13 years old, she told her family that she didn't want to go back to Haiti because she felt too unhappy about it. However, in her early twenties she went back to Haiti in order to become an activist:

> And that's where I first of all, started to learn Creole more and made my friendships with people who were journalists, who were progressives and people who were actively working against the Duvalier regime. And that's where I kind of ended up both doing my journalism and then of course writing the novel *Under the Bone*.[9]

D'Adesky's parents did not want to engage in politics. Growing up under the Duvalier regime, her family members did not want her to say anything about Duvalier[10] or the Tontons Macoutes. However, that did not sit well with her rebellious nature:

> I mean, to live in a dictatorship is something that it's so entrenched at every level, and for people who are trying to, it's a conceit to think you can remain apolitical in a dictatorship. You're either supporting the dictatorship or you're taking action against it.[11]

At a time when her family was trying to convince her not to do any reporting about politics in Haiti because it was too dangerous, she took a position against the dictatorship of the Duvalier regime: "So, when I did my journalism, I didn't even stay with my family. I was called a race traitor straight out, not because of the fact that they were racist. My family actually is not racist, but because they were so afraid of the repercussions and there were good reasons to be afraid."[12] Journalism was not the first item on the list of d'Adesky's studies. First, she was thinking about becoming an artist like her mother, after she entertained the idea of studying medicine. However, a series of events happened in her life that changed everything:

> My family was really having a struggle. So, I decided to stay in Florida rather than go up north to school. Initially. And at the time, my career goal was focused on tennis. I was going to be a tennis professional. I had been playing for years. I went to Rollins College on a tennis scholarship. I played basketball. I was very sporty. But I wasn't in any way dealing with my personal life. I didn't have any idea about my sexuality. I was very late.[13]

Raised in a conservative family, she had a hard time dealing with her sexuality:

> And what happened was I just had to eventually confront the fact that I guess I was a lesbian. But it took a very long time. It was, of course, the last thing I wanted to be because it meant that I would be losing my family, which is what happened. So, when I came out, my father was completely opposed and said, you're not going to be part of this family. He changed his mind later.[14]

That was a difficult period in her life. She felt rejected and abandoned by her family for a while. However, her trip to Paris after her mother's passing had a great impact on her life and helped propel her in a new direction. It was after receiving her bachelor's degree in arts and writing from Rollins College. Since she did not know what she wanted to do, one day, she went to spend time at the café in Paris called *Les deux Magots*. That is when she learned that this was a place where the renowned feminist writer Simon de Beauvoir and the philosopher Jean-Paul Sartre used to hang out. She was intrigued by what she learned about them:

> I liked not just the fact that they were public intellectuals and engaged against Stalin and had this circle of people, but also the fact that they lived one above the other and had this incredible social circle. And I thought, now there's a model. That's literally what my model was for what I wanted to do in my life. I wanted to be the two of them in their relationship.[15]

The reading of Simone de Beauvoir's second diary "Force of Circumstance" impacted her and changed her career. Talking about Simone de Beauvoir, d'Adesky mentioned that:

> I was so impressed by the fact that she had such a sense of purpose as an engaged writer. She had this incredible social circle. She was teaching, and most importantly, she was having an impact on her day and on her time. And I thought, that's what I'd like to do.[16]

Consumed by the desire to follow in the footsteps of Simone de Beauvoir, she entertained the idea of exploring journalism. That encouraged her to apply to Columbia University Graduate School of Journalism where she ultimately received a master's degree in 1982. However, after graduation, her dream of working for a prestigious newspaper did not materialize. As she explained:

> So, what I realized at Columbia School of Journalism is that I thought I wanted to be a writer for The New York Times, but The New York Times would not want me. I was already coming out. And even to be gay, to say you were gay, meant that you were considered to have an activist position, and you were not qualified to write for The New York Times. No one was out at that time. There were no outriders whatsoever.[17]

She really did not know what to do. Since she had been kicked out of her family, she thought the best thing to do was to write about what was in her circle. That is why she decided to write about what was going on in her local community, and most importantly, what was happening in Haiti, which was the beginning of the *dechoukaj*[18] movement. She used her connections to help her find information:

> I mean, all the people who are supporting the regime are friends of my family, so let me go and talk to them. So that's where I began doing my journalism, and I became a stringer for The San Francisco examiner, and I really began to do human rights reporting. It was a very exciting time, very dangerous. And I could see right away that, you know, my passport, my skin color, my class privilege, and my family name would allow me to bring in either my colleagues who were the Haitian journalists or I could ask the questions they wanted to ask that they maybe wouldn't get to ask in the room.[19]

So, d'Adesky used her privilege as a means to extract crucial information about the dictatorial government in Haiti. That is how she was able to monitor and cover human rights in Haiti. One day, by chance, when she found out that her name was on the "liste noire" ("Black list") to be killed by people working for the government, she left Haiti. And this was already in the period where Duvalier had been kicked out. During her stay in Haiti, she was conducting investigations, going to prisons, trying to find out what was happening with Fort Dimanche being the big killing fields, and particularly an area called Titanyen, which historically was the place where bodies were dumped. Her story about Titanyen, published in *The Village Voice*,[20] brought a lot more attention to Titanyen[21] and placed blame, and consequently, some lawsuits were presented. Since she could not publish all her multifaceted investigations about the Duvalier regime as well the military figures who were oppressing Haitians after the departure of Jean-Claude Duvalier, she decided to publish everything in a book. That is essentially the crux of *Under the Bone*. As mentioned by d'Adesky:

> So, *Under the Bone* was based on my feeling very strongly about the criminalization of ordinary Haitians who often were engaging in justice to try to call out an injustice like the characters in the book, but instead they themselves would be imprisoned. And then I also wanted to write a little bit about some of the issues, like the relations between Americans and Haitians, women and men and things.[22]

Her intimate familiarity with the Duvalier regime lent authenticity to her fictionalized depictions in *Under the Bone*. D'Adesky is an author who cannot keep quiet in the face of injustice and *Under the Bone* is her way of expressing her disgust for repression. She truly thinks that education can help people change their situations. According to her, "Our perspective on the past changes as we get more information, and therefore it's critical for us to examine the past. And in doing that, we shift the present and we change the future."[23] D'Adesky mentioned that:

> And when I spent so much time interviewing people in the prisons, which were just the worst conditions, as you can imagine, and very heartbreaking. I could sense how people survived. And I felt like it was one thing that I could give, that I wanted to make

people aware that while they were physically imprisoned and their bodies were being punished and they were literally shackled, they still were able to escape their minds and be in touch with their humanity and speak. Even if they're only speaking to their dead.[24]

Under the Bone

In *Under the Bone*, a book that d'Adesky dedicates to Duvalier's many deceased victims, the author explores post-Duvalier Haiti, by presenting characters whose mission consists of uncovering the truth about disappeared activists. Throughout the novel, she refers to numerous grave violations of human rights, illustrating the corruption and reign of terror that arose in Haitian society during both Duvalier regimes as well as their immediate aftermath. François Duvalier (1907–1971), known as Papa Doc, whose rule in Haiti began in 1957 and ended in 1971, and his son, Jean-Claude Duvalier (1951–2014), also known as Baby Doc, whose rule began in 1971 and ended in 1986, were proprietary dictators who ushered in an era of extreme brutality[25], corruption and fraud, particularly with the establishment of Papa Doc's private army, the Tontons Macoutes, in 1959. The putative purpose of this paramilitary unit, often referred to as Death squads, was to carry out the direct orders of Papa Doc, and later Baby Doc, in order to ensure full compliance among the people they ruled.

In *Under the Bone*, Anne-Christine d'Adesky presents a vivid depiction of women's experiences[26] under the Duvalier regimes. In addition to their documented aggressive and consistent assault on even basic human rights, anecdotal evidence suggests that these regimes were notorious for obfuscating any effort at releasing information that would condemn them. Women, particularly those belonging to the less privileged social classes, were doubly marginalized because of their gender and lack of power. The novel provides a compelling story about a particularly overlooked aspect of Haitian women's suffering, that of the unlawful, ruthless and secretive incarceration of women during the Duvalier regimes. D'Adesky states this focus rather explicitly since according to the novel's narrator, "No one had paid attention to the experience of women in Duvalier's prisons and what might still be happening to them"[27] (*Under the Bone*, 146).

The principal themes of the book are women's experiences, violence, silence, memory, and dreams.[28] D'Adesky applies le *métissage linguistique* by using four languages in the novel: English, Haitian Creole, French, and Spanish. Her use of Haitian Creole[29] is worthy of note as in spite of its momentous role in the founding and history of Haiti, it was only made one of the country's official languages in 1987.[30] D'Adesky's use of the various languages is often either a distancing mechanism, or one of closer social and affective association between characters.

The author's multilingual technique reflects a sampling of Haiti's population, and how the population interacted both internally and externally. The diverse characters include a grave-robbing driver, Catholic priests[31], medical doctors, lawyers, a laundress, unionists, and several middle to upper-class Haitians, all of whom have an opportunity to tell their story. Throughout the novel, this aforementioned variety of narrators confronts the reader with dissimilar or shifting narrative perspectives on life in Haiti shortly after the fall of Duvalierism, and thus clearly demonstrates the necessity for a multitude of different voices to construct a cohesive truth.

Under the Bone is, largely, a novel about the inquiry into women's conditions in Duvalier prisons. Its literary intent is signaled in the beginning of the novel, as the narrator states, "She [Leslie] wanted to visit Haiti again, to research an oral history project about women who had been imprisoned under the Duvaliers" (*Under the Bone*, 23). By apportioning significance to oral history, d'Adesky accentuates the difficulty of obtaining documents during the Duvalier years in Haiti. The scholar Paul Tiyambe Zeleza[32] made some remarks about how the oral tradition remains an important category among some female historian writers to uncover and recover women's experience. These remarks are applicable to d'Adesky's novel, "Feminist historians, more specifically, have embraced oral history as a key method to recover women's experiences and voices… it [oral history] creates new material about women, validates women's experience, enhances communication among women, discovers women's roots."[33] (Zeleza 219). In this instance, these oral accounts help provide information that is currently non-existent in archives or written documents.

Using oral history methods, journalistic and literary practices,[34] d'Adesky constructs a version of the extent of the oppression women suffered under the Duvaliers. One example is Marie-Thérèse Dubossy, who endures unjust persecution in a draft of a play written by Leslie's friend Gerard, who is also a human rights lawyer. In an interview with the Red Cross in 1986, Dubossy reveals her conditions in prison, the realities the prisoners face, and the government's politics of maintaining an unblemished self-portrait before the international community while oppressing political prisoners. In a paradoxical manner, women were sidelined, yet when it suited the dictatorships' purposes, the women were not only autonomous, but responsible for the actions of those around them as the scholar Carolle Charles remarked. (*Gender and Politics* 140) Dubossy speculates that she was arrested because her uncle had run against a Macoute in the municipal elections of 1979. (*Under the Bone*, 148).

In addition, Dubossy suffered humiliation under the hands of General Henri Lucerne. She was forced to strip and walk back and forth 50 times before General

Lucerne and his Macoute companions while they cursed and spit on her (*Under the Bone*, 149). Naturally, she also faced horrible living conditions in prison that included rats, mice, snails and cockroaches. (*Under the Bone*, 149–150). She was often beaten, and she almost lost an eye as a result. When she complained to the guards about the abuse, she was classified as a troublemaker. Dubossy relates that she was withdrawn from the prison to a clinic, an act that she qualifies as an attempt to fool the international community. The issue was that Baby Doc could only receive financial support from the United States as long as he did not hold political prisoners. Her transfer to that clinic is under false pretenses, as it was in fact an alternate prison: "They call it a medical clinic—an infirmary—but it did not really have any medicine or anything, just a bed." (*Under the Bone*, 149) Dubossy's testimony, though fictional, exposes the injustice women faced in prison in the sense that they were deprived of the right to seek a lawyer for their defense. Her story unveils the criminal politics of the Duvalier regimes throughout which prisons were generally a passage to Death; they either let you die out of hunger, or they killed you themselves.[35]

An additional example of how women were mistreated[36] can be gleaned in the character L'Esperance Fini, who is also from Gerard's play. Women were commonly arrested under false accusations during the Duvalier period, and L'Esperance Fini (character in Gerard's play) was a woman who died in prison after being detained for years without a trial. Some accounts alleged that she was accused of stealing china from the Minister of Recreation, but this turned out to be false. A letter that she addressed to her mother revealed a different reason for her arrest, that she would not succumb to the Minister's sexual[37] advances. (*Under the Bone*, 297) It is clear here that L'Esperance Fini has been arrested because she refused to engage in a sexual relationship with the Minister of Recreation, which was a common practice among the Macoutes. Whenever women rejected their advances, they charged them with a crime and had them put in jail.[38]

Under the Bone addresses the ferocity and bloodthirsty behavior of the Tontons Macoutes, as best demonstrated by the improper imprisonment of the character Elyse Voltaire upon her discovery of a corpse. The authorities arrested Elyse because they wished to tie her to a crime. In addition to her gender, social class and youth, Elyse's vulnerability is highlighted by the fact that as a pregnant woman in prison, she did not receive proper nutrition: "My stomach isn't growing though, because they don't give us enough food. And what they give us is so bad that I can't even swallow it. So, I force myself. I have to stay strong for the baby" (*Under the Bone*, 104). The Macoutes' attempt to cover up this murder for which they are responsible directly violated Elyse's right to a fair trial and completely flouted the country's justice system, thus emphasizing the rampant depravity and lack of governmental infrastructure in Haiti at that time. The story continues, by disclosing that Elyse's stand against paying arbitrarily raised taxes played a significant role in her incarceration. (*Under the Bone*, 9). Her actions highlight the bravery and strategy of a woman who challenged her colleagues to defy the state. Although she was accused of assaulting a military officer, the real motive for her arrest was that she refused to pay taxes on the water they used.

The imprisonment of women remains a domain through which it becomes manifest that Haitian women are not passive, but rather have resisted political oppression. The character Edith can be used as an example of a woman who resisted the dictatorial regime and suffered as a result. As the narrator describes her: "Edith was considered one of the outspoken women in the country, far more radical than most unionists." (*Under the Bone*, 129–130) Her stand against the Duvalier exploitation and oppression of workers and peasants causes her imprisonment. However, Edith's experience in prison makes her more determined than ever in her struggle for social justice. As the narrator points out: "She had been arrested three times in the past six years, and beaten once, though not badly. But each incident, rather than silencing her, sharpened her tongue. She was not afraid to denounce the regime." (*Under the Bone*, 130). In the struggle for social justice, not only does she criticize the government's policy, but she also mobilizes people to get involved in strikes: shopkeepers, students, and peasants etc. Her stance against the Duvalier exploitation and the oppression of workers and peasants was remarkable. Her activism, prison experience and energetic resistance to the Duvalier regimes suggest that the gender characterization of political oppression and resistance was subverted through the work of these women.[39]

Conclusion

In conclusion, d'Adesky's work transcends any single approach, applying autobiographical, philosophical, and psychoanalytic approaches. Her linguistic choice is of great importance, because English brings her work into the venue to publicize the injustices of Haiti for the Anglophone world. It is not an exaggeration to say that her novel transcends linguistic, territorial, and critical approaches. In other words, it is part of a cross-disciplinary conversation. As the renowned author of historical fiction, Maryse Condé, suggested, women's involvement in writing brings about a literary parody she refers to as "disorder," because women's writings shake the foundation of masculine writers, thus creating counter-canonical literary productions. Women writers characterize heroines, center actions around female characters, reveal the true experience of women, and restore women's historicity. This is clearly the case with *Under the Bone*.

Notes

1. Holden, Sue. Reviewed work(s): "Moving Mountains: The Race to Treat Global AIDS" by Anne-Christine d'Adesky. *Development in Practice*, Vol. 15, No. 1 (Feb., 2005), pp. 126–128.
2. McGough, Laura J. Reviewed Work(s): Moving Mountains: The Race to Treat Global AIDS by Anne-Christine D'Adesky. Bulletin of the History of Medicine, Vol. 79, No 3 (Fall 2005), pp. 617–618.
3. Ibid., 617.
4. Kahn, Karen. Reviewed Work(s): "Moving Mountains: The Race to Treat Global AIDS" by Anne-Christine d'Adesky. *The Women's Review of Books*, Dec., 2004, Vol. 22, No. 3 (Dec., 2004), pp. 24–25.
5. Michel, Claudine. *Journal of Haitian Studies*. Vol. 19, No. 2, Special Issue on Michel-Rolph Trouillot. Fall 2013.
6. <https://www.skylightbooks.com/event/anne-christine-dadesky-discusses-her-book-pox-lover-councilmember-lindsey-horvath>
7. Anne-Christine d'Adesky. Interview with Wedsly Turenne Guerrier. Brooklyn. October 6, 2023.
8. Ibid.
9. Ibid.
10. In her 1984 article entitled "Woman Catalyst to Haiti Uprising," d'Adesky argues that the movement to overthrow President Jean-Claude Duvalier started by a woman resisting the order of a Tonton in the city of Gonaives. (d'Adesky, "Woman Catalyst," p.4).

    D'Adesky, Anne-Christine. "Woman Catalyst to Haitian Uprising." *Woman News*. NYC Feminist Newspaper. July/August 1984. pp. 4–5.
11. Anne-Christine d'Adesky. Interview with Wedsly Turenne Guerrier. Brooklyn. October 6, 2023.
12. Ibid.
13. Ibid.
14. Ibid.
15. Ibid.
16. Ibid.
17. Ibid.
18. According to Arthur and Dash: "In the months following Duvalier's departure, this embryonic popular movement focused on the attempt to eradicate the most visible manifestations of the Duvalier regime-a process known as *dechoukaj*, or uprooting." (p. 143).

    Charles, Arthur and Dash, Michael. *A Haiti Anthology: Libète*. Markus Wiener Publishers, 1999.
19. Anne-Christine D'Adesky. Interview with Wedsly Turenne Guerrier. Brooklyn. October 6, 2023.
20. D'Adesky, Anne-Christine. "The Bones of Haiti." *Village Voice*, June 11, 1991.
21. The critic Suzanne Ruta argues that: "The villagers of Titanyen, a killing field deep in the countryside, are impotent witnesses to massacre. Against the silence of the terrorized, the discouraged, the indifferent, the uninformed, d'Adesky has written a courageous and provocative appeal." (Ruta, p. 3)

Ruta, Suzanne. Reviewed Work (s): Under the Bone by Anne-Christine d'Adesky: Breath, Eyes, Memory by Edwidge Danticat. The Women's Review of Books. Oct. 1994, Vol. 12, No. 1, (Oct., 1994), pp. 1+3.

22 Anne-Christine d'Adesky. Interview with Wedsly Turenne Guerrier. Brooklyn. October 6, 2023.

23 Ibid.

24 Ibid.

25 Myriam Chancy notes that "The reason Duvalier's reign of terror took on cataclysmic proportions was that anyone, regardless of race, sex, class, age, or political affiliation, could become its victim." (*Framing Silence*, p.147).

26 According to Myriam Chancy, *with Under the Bone*, d'Adesky seeks "to express a feminist and women-identified politics." (*Framing Silence*, p.22).

27 D'Adesky, Anne-Christine. *Under the Bone*. New York: Farrar, Straus and Giroux, 1994.

28 The scholar Myriam Chancy argues that "In d'Adesky's novel women attempt to overcome silence through dreams that reconnect them to one another and that reimbue them with a sense of hope about the world, even as the society about them denies their oppression. The imagination serves as the outlet for regeneration rather than desperation." (*Framing Silence*, p.144, 145).

Chancy, Myriam J. A. *Framing Silence: Revolutionary Novels by Haitian Women*. Rutgers University Press, 1997.

29 Talking about Creole, d'Adesky mentioned that: "I also think that the language carries culture, and I felt it was really important, particularly with Voodoo, where the songs that my friends and people close to me who helped to be around me would sing. I felt I wanted to give honor to those songs and that experience. I wanted to show that it was a religious and spiritual tradition of resistance and survival and culture. So, I wanted it to be in there for that reason, a combination of both honoring and also because that is the language being spoken by some of the characters in the book who don't have the privilege of having been educated to maybe write or read. So those were all important reasons for me."

Anne-Christine d'Adesky. Interview with Wedsly Turenne Guerrier. Brooklyn. October 6, 2023.

30 For more information, see article 5 of the 1987 Constitution of Haiti. <https://pdba.georgetown.edu/Constitutions/Haiti/constitution1987en.pdf>

31 D'Adesky mentioned that she added the priest character because "While the elite was being very targeted and while political activists were targeted, the people who were deeply targeted in places like *Artibonite* and all the way across *Papaye* and everything were teachers, were educators and priests. And one reason was because that's where people went to gather in schools and Churches. So that's where the dictatorship was trying to kill a progressive or democratic spirit. And so, I wanted to have that character. That was my reason." D'Adesky, Anne-Christine. Interview with Wedsly Turenne Guerrier. Brooklyn. October 6, 2023.

32 Paul Tiyambe Zeleza is a Malawian historian, literary critic, novelist, short-story writer and blogger at The Zeleza Post. He was president of the African Studies Association.

33 Zeleza, Paul Tiyambe. "Gender Biases in African Historiography." *Oyěwùmí O. (eds) African Gender Studies: A Reader*. New York: Palgrave Macmillan, 2005.

34 According to Kathleen Sheldon, it is, in fact, the combination of archives and oral testimony that makes the research and recovery of women's history efficient (Sheldon, 480).

Sheldon, Kathleen. "Writing about Women: Approaches to a Gendered Perspective in African History." *Writing African History*. Edited by John Edward Philips. By Bala Achi et al., Boydell & Brewer, 2005, pp. 465–490.

[35] For more information, see d'Adesky, Anne-Christine. "The Bones of Haiti." *Village Voice*, June 11, 1991.

[36] Elyse, one of the characters in *Under the Bone*, becomes one of many in the crowded prison in Port-au-Prince, where she meets a Dominican woman, Luz, who has been brutally beaten because of her activities as a prostitute, to which she resorted in order to feed her children: "The policeman had beaten her up before arresting her. Elyse had understood that much of the woman's story. He had refused to pay Luz for sex; she had protested and now she was in here and her children were out there." (*Under the Bone*, 61)

[37] Ginette Adamson argues that patriarchal literary works portray the woman as an object of desire for men. ("De fonds Rouge à Port-au-Prince : une représentation de l'haïtienne," p. 46). Adamson, Ginette. "De fonds rouge à Port-au-Prince : Une représentation de l'haïtienne : discours masculin-discours féminin," *Nouvelles Écritures féminines : la parole aux femmes*, Paris, Notre librairie N.17, 1994, pp. 44–47.

[38] In her article "Woman Catalyst to Haitian Uprising," d'Adesky argues that "In a country marked by political corruption, women there are particularly vulnerable to attacks by the Macoutes, who govern with impunity and violence. Reports of women raped by the Macoutes are not uncommon, nor are the exchanges of sex to avoid arrest or even Death; in addition, they are made the scapegoat for actions by their husbands, lovers, fathers, and sons." (d'Adesky, "Woman Catalyst," p. 4). D'Adesky, Anne-Christine. "Woman Catalyst to Haitian Uprising." *Woman News*. NYC Feminist Newspaper. July/August 1984. pp. 4–5.

[39] Edith's activism and her prison experience supports Charles' argument that "Under the Duvalierist state, however, systemic repressive policies undermined the prevailing conception of women as passive political actors, devoted mothers, and political innocents." (Charles, 138). Charles, Carolle. "Gender and Politics in Contemporary Haiti: The Duvalierist State, Transnationalism, and the Emergence of a New Feminism (1980–1990)." *Feminist Studies*, Vol. 21, No. 1 (Spring, 1995), pp. 135–164.

Bibliography

Adamson, Ginette. "De fonds rouge à Port-au-Prince : Une représentation de l'haïtienne : discours masculin-discours féminin," *Nouvelles Écritures féminines : la parole aux femmes*, Paris, Notre librairie N.17, 1994, pp. 44–47.

Chancy, Myriam J. A. *Framing Silence: Revolutionary Novels by Haitian Women*. Rutgers University Press, 1997.

Charles, Carolle. "Gender and Politics in Contemporary Haiti: The Duvalierist State, Transnationalism, and the Emergence of a New Feminism (1980–1990)." *Feminist Studies*, Vol. 21, No. 1 (Spring, 1995), pp. 135–164.

D'Adesky, Anne-Christine. *Beyond Shock: Charting the Landscape of Sexual Violence I Post-quake Haiti*. CBSR and HSA, 2013.

———. Interview with Wedsly Turenne Guerrier. Brooklyn. October 6, 2023.

———. *Moving Mountains: The Race to Treat Global AIDS*. Verso, 2004.

———. "The Bones of Haiti." *The Village Voice*. June 11, 1991.

———. *The Pox Lover: An Activist's Decade in New York and Paris*. Wisconsin: University of Wisconsin Press, 2017.

———. *Under the Bone*. New York: Farrar, Straus and Giroux, 1994.

———. "Woman Catalyst to Haitian Uprising." *Woman News*. NYC Feminist Newspaper. July/August 1984. pp. 4–5.

Holden, Sue. Reviewed work(s): "Moving Mountains: The Race to Treat Global AIDS" by Anne-Christine d'Adesky. *Development in Practice*, Vol. 15, No. 1 (Feb., 2005), pp. 126–128.

Kahn, Karen. Reviewed Work(s): "Moving Mountains: The Race to Treat Global AIDS" by Anne-Christine d'Adesky. *The Women's Review of Books*, Dec., 2004, Vol. 22, No. 3 (Dec., 2004), pp. 24–25.

McGough, Laura J. Reviewed Work(s): Moving Mountains: The Race to Treat Global AIDS by Anne-Christine d'Adesky. Bulletin of the History of Medicine, Vol. 79, No 3 (Fall 2005), pp. 617–618.

Michel, Claudine. *Journal of Haitian Studies*. Vol. 19, No. 2, Special Issue on Michel-Rolph Trouillot. Fall 2013.

Ruta, Suzanne. Reviewed Work (s): Under the Bone by Anne-Christine d'Adesky: Breath, Eyes, Memory by Edwidge Danticat. The Women's Review of Books. Oct. 1994, Vol. 12, No. 1, (Oct., 1994), pp. 1+3.

Sheldon, Kathleen. "Writing about Women: Approaches to a Gendered Perspective in African History." *Writing African History*. Edited by John Edward Philips. By Bala Achi et al., Boydell & Brewer, 2005, pp. 465–490.

Zeleza, Paul Tiyambe. "Gender Biases in African Historiography." Oyěwùmí O. (eds) *African Gender Studies: A Reader*. New York: Palgrave Macmillan, 2005.

CHAPTER 5

Jean-Claude Martineau: Songs as Cautionary Tales

Introduction

Jean-Claude Martineau (1937–X) is a Haitian songwriter, storyteller, playwright, activist, statesman and historian who has worked tirelessly on a mission to facilitate his compatriots to think critically about Haitian culture.[1] He aims to move people to appreciate Haiti and Haitian culture on its own terms as opposed to rejecting it because of conscious or unconscious acceptance of the negative depictions of Haiti through various forms of international media. Through his endeavors, he has shown the roots of some of Haiti's misfortunes and their effects on the Haitian people both at home and in the diaspora. His writing captures the reader's attention with his sense of humor and his ability to inspire people to come to their own conclusions about what it means, on a deep level, to be Haitian and/or to value Haitian identity and its ethos. This chapter will present an overview of Martineau's biography and analyze one of his songs, "*Vyewo*." I will show the context in which the song was written and highlight the messages that can be drawn from it.

Biography of Jean-Claude Martineau

In introducing the book *Flè dizè: Powèm, chante* (1982), the scholar Marika Roumain provides crucial information about Martineau's biography. According to her, Jean-Claude Martineau was born on January 27, 1937, in Croix-Des-Bouquets, Haiti. Since his father came from the South (Jérémie) and his mother from the North (Plaisance), he was familiar with an extensive range of Haitian culture. As rural teachers, his parents often moved to different towns to teach, which permitted the young Martineau to become acquainted with Haitian folklore and the lives of peasants. At an early age, around 16, he started writing poetry in

French, though later his medium of expression became Haitian Creole. Martineau graduated from High School in Lycée Toussaint L'Ouverture in Port-au-Prince. According to the critic Jean Numa Foudou, Jean-Claude Martineau wanted to be an agronomist, but could not attend the agronomy school because the school accepted a new promotion of students only every four years. Since he was not in a position to wait this time, he studied accounting instead.[2] He also worked at a Port-au-Prince radio station for seven years, in various capacities, and even hosted his own show at one point. Since radio is such a critical component of Haitian life, it was through this work that he began promoting a message of unity.

In 1950, Martineau attended the poet Félix Morisseau-Leroy's (1912–1998) reading of a poem in Haitian Creole, which inspired him to follow suit.[3] In 1962[4], he moved[5] to the United States. According to the scholar Statler Luczama: "A fan of freedom of expression, he joined the movements against the dictatorial regime in the late 1960s, and was forced to leave his homeland to settle in the United States. Nostalgic, he found an immeasurable refuge in theater, writing and music, all of which eventually became synchronized in his artistic heritage."[6] By 1971, he was deeply involved in the Haitian diaspora. In Boston, for example, he composed poems, songs, and plays for the group called "Haïti Culturelle."[7] Whenever there was a Haitian event, he was always present, whether in New York, Boston, Montréal, Philadelphia, or Miami. In response to my question about the performance group *Haïti Culturelle*, Martineau mentions:

> Well, we were fighting against the dictatorship of Duvalier, and the Haitian population was still very scared. We wanted to sell them newspapers, and they didn't care about that. They were too afraid of Duvalier. So, we decided to use our culture to connect with and move them. So that's how *Haïti Culturelle* was created. Through *Haïti Culturelle*, we started singing, writing plays and staging them, and holding conferences about the situation of women in Haiti and the situation of the children in Haiti and things like that. And little by little, we started attracting people. *Haïti Culturelle* was created in order to help us mobilize the community.[8]

Martineau composed many songs and plays in Boston. By 1982, he had recorded more than 22 songs. Among his most famous ones are: "*Lè l'a libere Ayiti va bèl o!*," "*Mawoule*," "*Li-Jan Boje*," and "*Vyewo*." In an interview granted to the journalist Fred Williams[9], he offered many reasons why he believes that writing in Haitian Creole is important. He stressed that some people in Haiti subscribe to the antiquated elitist belief that poetry is not made for everyone[10] and that only French must be used to compose this literary genre. Such a view prevents millions of Haitians from accessing poetry and writing poetry themselves. He also mentioned that he wrote in Creole in order to speak on behalf of a nation that has the potential to understand his message. In addition, he is particularly adept at demonstrating how Creole is a beautifully expressive language that easily lends itself to poetic manifestation. Martineau mentioned why using Haitian Creole in his work is important: "Well, I started writing about Haitian Creole when describing the work that we wanted to do in *Haiti Culturelle*, because we couldn't mobilize the community with any other language than their own. So that's exactly why we started, not me alone, but a lot of us, we started writing in Creole."[11] He taught Haitian culture at Roxbury Community College before becoming a cultural attaché in the Boston consulate. In 1991, after the coup d'état against President Aristide (1953–...), Martineau was transferred to the Haitian Embassy in Washington because he was an Aristide ally.

In 1994, Martineau returned to Haiti to work at the National Television of Haiti, presenting a program about Education. In discussing his work at the National Television of Haiti, Martineau stated the following:

> I was there to replace somebody who was responsible for the section of culture on television. He went to the United States for a while, and then I became the director of the cultural section. And when he came back, I gave him back his position, but I stayed on national TV and in the Department of Culture.[12]

Martineau is an artist who is beloved in Haiti as well as in the Haitian diaspora. One of his most famous songs, "*Ayiti Demen*," has been interpreted by many Haitian artists and is well appreciated in the Haitian community. It projects a future in which Haitians will be free from dictatorship as well as foreign influence, and Haiti will flourish as a nation. The battle will be hard, but step by step, Haitians will achieve a destiny that they richly deserve but has thus far escaped them. In realizing the influence of Martineau's songs in the Haitian community, The Scholar Danielle Legros Georges notes:

> His texts are sung, read on the radio, performed as plays, and recited by heart by Haitian schoolchildren. He has created several anthems of Haitian liberation including "*Ayiti Demen (Lè la libéré Ayiti va bèl)*" written in 1978 against the backdrop of the almost thirty-year Duvalier dictatorship.[13]

The critic Robert Maguire in his article titled "Toward the End of Poverty in Haiti," mentions that "In July 2006, Haitian poet and historian Jean-Claude Martineau spoke at USIP[14] and said that Haiti is the only country in the world with a last name—'Haiti, poorest country in the western hemisphere' —as described in the media."[15] Martineau firmly believes that there is an international campaign to cast Haiti in a negative light. He makes it his life-long mission to encourage Haitians to counteract the negative propaganda spread about their country.

CHAPTER 5

He is an author and activist who is not afraid to criticize what he sees as his fellow Haitians' shortcomings. He often proposes possible solutions. For instance, in his article titled "Haitian Culture: Basis for Haiti's Development" published in 1996, (see Arthur and Dash, 245) Martineau deplores the invasion of western traditions in Haiti through television and the radio: "Meanwhile, there is no program about our cuisine, our medicinal herbs, and plants, our fruits, our theater, our folktales... If instead of consuming locally produced goods we are bombarded with images of foreign goods, we are doomed."[16] (Quoted in Arthur and Dash, 245) He subscribes to the notion that Haitians should be proud of their history, respect their traditions, and make a point of encompassing their shared culture. According to him, Haitian culture should be an inclusive part of any debate about Haiti's future Development. In many of his works, Martineau describes the tremendous efforts made by ordinary Haitians to improve their lives whether in Haiti or abroad. It is in that context that Legros Georges, in her article "Jean-Claude Martineau: Poet of the Underdog" mentions the following:

> Jean-Claude Martineau is a poet of the underdog. Throughout a long career as a writer (as well as songwriter, composer, activist, and statesperson), Martineau has made visible the experiences of Haitians who fight on Haitian soil and in its diaspora to uphold their right to self-determination and human dignity—often against great odds, and in defiance of great powers.[17]

One of Martineau's multiple gifts is his sensitivity, his ability to invent a story and make readers feel, on a personal level, what the characters are enduring. In reading his works, the reader is particularly drawn in and feels as though an emotional journey is taking place in which it is effortless to experience what the characters are facing while reflecting on one's life. Realizing the impact of some of Martineau's works on the reader, Legros Georges argues that:

> We see the ten-year-old orphan who fends for himself while dreaming of attending school in the poem *"Diver."* We identify with the narrator's concern for this child. In "I'll Roll Along," we walk the night in the Haitian countryside with the cow herder who teaches us a lesson of perseverance and collaboration.[18]

His influence in Haiti as well as in the Haitian diaspora is noticeable. On April 15, 1997, the founder of Radio Haiti Inter, the agronomist and journalist Jean Dominique had an interview with Jean-Claude Martineau in which they discussed Haitian language and culture. During this exchange:

> Jean-Claude Martineau (*Koralen*) discusses the need to valorize Haitian culture amid an invasion of foreign (particularly US) cultural influence. Haitian people are taught

that American food, music, and films are better than anything Haiti produces. They spend their money on cornflakes rather than eating cassava[19], *lalo*, or rice and beans; they consume films that glamorize sex, cars, drugs, and guns; they wear *pèpè* clothes rather than buying Haitian-made clothing. And so Haitian money does not stay in Haiti; it flows to other countries. Martineau underlines the need for Haiti to export its products, not only to import.[20]

As a keen observer, Martineau analyzes the way that Haitians live and their tendencies to gravitate toward foreign-made products instead of their own. According to him, when discussing culture, songs and plays are not the only items to take into consideration. He stresses that many people ignore the fact that culture has an economic aspect to it which can lead to Development. He maintains that Haitians should be shown films that can teach them something about themselves. He complains about the violent nature of many films that have nothing to do with Haitians. He laments the fact that in many restaurants, hotels, even in cars, foreign music abounds. In discussing Haitian music, Martineau argues that "We refuse to exploit it, we refuse to present it. We refuse to say musically who we are, what we do, what we say."[21] He mentions a mental occupation that Haitians would do well to eliminate. For example, Haitians refuse to eat local products and instead spend lots of money on imported food. He complains that many Haitians subscribe to the false notion that what is made in Haiti is no good. He calls for local production and argues that "Whatever is fabricated in the country [Haiti] will allow money to flow and will be less expensive. Unfortunately, there is no real effort to make us love what is ours, to adopt what is ours, and to work with what belongs to us."[22] He is convinced that there will be no accumulation of wealth if Haitians keep spending their money in foreign countries. Thus, one could argue that on some level it is a perpetuation of a colonial economy. Martineau complains that small merchants who are trying to make a living don't have access to credit which could not only help them expand their commerce but create jobs as well. Martineau exposes the lack of infrastructure that prevents many of the local products from reaching other parts of the country. He encourages Haitians to get together in order to make Haiti a market for Haitians. He suggests that those who are making deals on behalf of the nation should consider the nation's interest in all negotiations. It is about time that Haitians start importing their goods to other nations. In the interview between Jean-Claude Martineau and Jean Dominique "They discuss the Haitian elite, the majority of whom have not done anything to improve the country. Pressure to change society will have to come from below."[23] When I asked Martineau why he writes so much about Haiti and Haitians, he laughed and said: "There is something that I always say, if I were a bricklayer, I would use that to serve my people. If I were a doctor,

I would use my profession to help the people. I am basically a patriot. Since I am a writer and some people like my writing, I use my work to serve my people."[24]

Analysis of "Vyewo"

The song that I analyze below comes from the book *Flè Dizè: Powèm chante*, published in New York in 1982. It is a collection of songs and poems written in Haitian Creole, French, and English. The first four pages are dedicated to the official Haitian Creole alphabet and a brief description of the book's contents. This shows Martineau's commitment to fostering the use of Haitian Creole at a time when many people doubted the literary possibilities of the language.

It is worthy of mention that Haitian Creole became one of the official languages of Haiti in 1987. However, historically, the use of Haitian Creole in music was widespread. Music plays a particularly poignant role in the fabric of Haitian culture. Much is communicated via songs, whether it is protest, revolution, strikes, religious ceremonies, or carnival. These songs provoke varying reactions-some songs produce tearful reactions whereas others make people laugh. Whatever the style, a song is never insignificant; it always carries a message. One wonders about Martineau's thematic choices and their significance in this song. He seems to challenge the trope of a promised land outside of Haiti, but nonetheless close to it. It is well known that many Haitians migrated either forcefully or not, in search of better economic opportunities. In order to contextualize Martineau's song, it is helpful to address the political, social, and economic processes in Haiti that contributed to migration in 1982. The main causes of migration were low wages, high unemployment rates, a lack of healthcare, a low standard of living, and widespread police brutality. Many Haitians from all sectors of life were running away from the Duvalier regime that was oppressing them. Some people were arrested without warrants, condemned without trials, tortured, and even killed. The Tontons Macoutes were a Haitian paramilitary force created in 1959 by President François Duvalier (1907–1971), or "Papa Doc." The Macoutes typically took prisoners to the Fort Dimanche prison where much torture was carried out, and if prisoners died, they were taken to the inaccessible Titanyen graveyard so that their families could not retrieve their bodies. To many Haitians, Haiti was a place to avoid. Some even sold all of their assets to escape torture and persecution. Others left because of poverty. Moreover, in the 1970s, famine struck, affecting the poor working class of northern Haiti. As the scholar James Ferguson puts it,

> The famine of the mid-1970s underlined the appalling poverty which existed in Haiti, particularly among the majority of Black subsistence farmers in the provinces. It also

JEAN-CLAUDE MARTINEAU

added impetus to the process of escape and voluntary exile, which was one of the most striking features of Baby Doc's presidency.[25] (Ferguson, 63)

In a country where there were not enough jobs for workers, life, and even mere survival, was complicated. So, in search of better economic opportunities, poor Haitians left the country in great numbers. Many took boats to Miami; others chose to go to the Dominican Republic instead.[26] The two interlocutors in *"Vyewo"*[27] are two Haitian peasant workers in search of a better life in the Dominican Republic and work as sugar cane cutters there.

While reading the lyrics, one notices the lack of punctuation: there is no period, but six commas. The absence of punctuation signals the flow of the conversation, just like a river. At the end of the song, there is an illustration of a big machete at the center of the second page. It signals the significance of such an instrument in the workers' lives. In that poem, we notice the Haitian Creole spelling of the early 1980s: *youn* (for yon), *oun* (for on) and the use of the apostrophe between nouns and possessive adjectives, between a vowel and marker starting with a vowel. These indicate that the poet followed to the letter the official orthography of the Creole language based on the September 18, 1979 law / decree.

Written in Haitian Creole and divided into three strophes, this song honestly depicts the arduous, gloomy lives of two poor Haitian workers living in a sugarcane plantation, called a *batey*[28], in the Dominican Republic. Although the song consists of three strophes, it can be divided into five parts. Each one brings another dimension to the narration. The narrator, through direct speech, reports the conversation between the two men. A *vyewo* is a Haitian cane cutter in the Dominican Republic who has lots of experience, contrary to the *kongo*, who has just arrived at the bateyes. The first strophe[29] sets the scene by providing ample information about the location[30] (*batèy, Higuèy, Dominicani*) in which such a conversation takes place. It also describes the physical conditions of the two men. The translation of the lyrics cited below is by Nadève Ménard.[31]

Nan mitan youn chan kann bò "Higwèy"
　An Dominikani
De Ayisyen chita nan oun batèy
　Pye atè do touni
Younn ape pale, younn ape koute
　Yo pa fè bri
Van nan kann nan sèlman ki tande
　Sa y'ape di (Martineau, page 65)

In the middle of a cane field near Higuey
In the Dominican Republic

CHAPTER 5

> Two Haitians sit in a batey,
> Barefoot and bare-chested.
> One is talking, one is listening
> They are not loud.
> The wind in the cane alone hears
> What they have to say. (Ménard, 284)

The expression "*De ayisyen chita*" signals a friendship and the word "*Batèy*" evokes a place of hard labor and interminable fatigue. The two men are probably taking a break from work. In the expression "*Younn ape pale, younn ape koute,*" the assonance, the repetition of the vowel "e," provides a certain rhythm to the text and creates an effect of insistence. From the first strophe, one discerns that the two interlocutors' lack of clothes—"*pye atè*" (no shoes), "*do touni*" (no t-shirts)—highlights their poverty. The narrator takes the time to emphasize that their conversation is so intimate that only the wind in the cane field can hear them. Songs, like poetry, allow us to communicate some impressions or correspondences between a sound and an impression. In the first line of the strophe mentioned above, there is an assonance or repetition of the nasal vowel "*an*": "*Nan mitan youn chan kann bò Igwèy.*" That nasal vowel, which expresses slowness and softness, underlines the peaceful atmosphere in which the conservation is taking place. The mention of the supple wind amplifies the idea of calmness: "*Van nan kann nan sèlman ki tande.*" The wind, which is personified, is a witness to the conversation.

The second part introduces the mission that the friend wants *vjewo* to accomplish on his behalf:

> *Vyewo, ou k'ap fè tè Ayiti*
> *Men oun komisyon w'a bay madanm mwen pou mwen*
> *Vyewo se oun "Diez peso"*
> *Vyewo avèk oun pè zanno*
> *Lè ou rive si ou jwenn li plase*
> *W'a bay manman mwen-l yo pou mwen* (Page 65)

> Vyewo, you who are going to work the land in Haiti,
> Here is something to give to my wife for me.
> Vyewo, it's "diez peso,"
> and a pair of earrings.
> When you get there, if she's living with someone else,
> You can give them to my mother. (Ménard, 284)

In the line, "*Men oun komisyon w'a bay madanm mwen pou mwen,*" we notice three nasal vowels "*en*," "*on*," and "*an*." These bright sounds are related to enthusiasm. They express the man's excitement about sending something to his family.

One of the interlocutors gives the *vyewo* "*Diez peso*" "ten pesos" and "*oun pè zanno*" a "pair of earrings" to give to his wife. The money ("*Diez peso*") is used in quotation marks to underline the unimportance of such an amount of money. These two gifts symbolize the most that the husband has to offer his wife back home. The reader quickly understands that his trip to the Dominican Republic has been a failure because what the husband can provide to his wife is so insignificant. Although the husband cannot afford to send a lot of money or expensive gifts back home to his wife he sends something to make his wife feel that he is still committed to the relationship. The other sorrowful part of the story is that he has nothing to send his mother,[32] which is why he kindly demands that the *vyewo* deliver the gifts to his mother[33] instead of his wife if the latter is with another man.[34] From that, we can conclude that the *vyewo* has a double mission: to carry a message and to spy on his friend's wife. How will the *vyewo* really find out if his friend's wife is cheating? It is not clear in the song how, but his role is to just find out. It is obvious that the husband is insecure about his wife. The distance between them, coupled with the time spent away from each other, makes the husband question his wife's faithfulness. It is fair to say that the husband and his wife have different perspectives regarding their family. While the husband focuses on material things and, in part, his assumed jealousy, his wife concentrates on the well-being of their children.

The third part, without providing any type of period, relates that the friend went and came back from Haiti. Although we do not have much information about when the trip that took place, what is obvious is that *vyewo* comes back with bad news:

Vyewo ale, vyewo tounen
Avèk nouvèl ki bay kè plen
Manman-an mouri
Sa gen kèk lannen
Gen moun ki di
Ke se chagren
Madanm nan la, l'ape kenbe
Men timoun yo mal okipe
Premye-a grandi tankou chwal
Ti dènye-a pa menm sonje papa-l

Vyewo went, Vyewo came back
With news that made the heart heavy.
The mother had died
Several years back.
Some people say
She died of sadness.

> The wife is still there,
> Still holding on,
> But the kids are not well cared for.
> The first one grew like a horse,
> The last one doesn't even remember his father. (Ménard, 284–285)

In the sentence "*Avèk nouvèl ki bay kè plen*," the alliteration, the repetition of the harsh sound "k" creates a feeling of hardness and suggests a difficult news to deal with. In Haitian Creole "*nouvèl ki bay kè plen*" means, a news that makes someone lose his/her appetite. This strophe reveals more information about the family left in Haiti. The cherished mother did not live long enough to see her son again. She was also unable to receive help from him. People believe that she died of chagrin: "*gen moun ki di / se chagren*." That gives us a taste of the Haitian culture. When someone dies in Haiti, anecdotal evidence shows that people usually speculate about the cause of Death. They don't wait for the result of an autopsy to find out what happened. It is important to point out that dying of chagrin has deleterious social consequences in some communities. Haitians are very close to their mothers, who are the central pillar of the family. In the Haitian community, in my experience, there is a belief that children are supposed to care for their parents as they age because the government has no structure in place to care for the elderly. The husband who could not care for his mother learns that she passed away in his absence. That is devastating news. This song emphasizes that leaving one's country is a risky adventure, an imperfect and largely ineffective solution at best. Many Haitian migrants spend their lives abroad in grueling situations trying to make a living, but they do not know how the families they left behind are faring or if their relatives are even still alive. The only news that the man is happy to receive is that his wife has remained faithful to him: "*Madanm nan la, l'ape kenbe*." This information is particularly revealing. It is assumed that, even if the husband is away for a long time, the wife is supposed to stay true to him. However, there are often differences between perceived behaviors and those that are realized. Martineau is referencing this. Temptation, peer pressure, depression, and alcohol can possibly induce sexual activities. In a poor country such as Haiti, it is easy for men of wealth to pursue poor married women in order to have sexual relations with them. The wife in this song, despite her poverty, disappointment, and false hope, stayed true to her husband, which says a lot about her resilience, perseverance, and self-control.

Although there was the welcome news of his wife's fidelity, there was undesirable news as well. The children are not well fed. The first one is growing like a wild horse, which is to say that he is out of control. The last child has no memory of his father. Misbehaving children can be due to the emotional impact of an absent father. The fact that there is no father figure in the house causes the first child to be insolent. The wife insinuates that it is not a good idea for a woman to raise children by herself. While the husband is away from his family, many things happen that he cannot witness. That is, frankly, a picture of a dysfunctional family.

In the fourth part, we notice a big change about nature:

> *Nan mitan youn chan kann bò "Higwèy"*
>   *An Dominikani*
> *De Ayisyen chita nan oun batèy*
>   *Pye atè, do touni*
> *Younn ape pale, Younn ap koute*
>   *Yo pa fè bri*
> *Van nan kann nan kouri efase*
>   *Sa y'ape di*

> In the middle of a cane field near Higuey
> In the Dominican Republic
> Two Haitians sit in a batey,
> Barefoot and bare-chested.
> One is talking, one is listening.
> They are not loud.
> The wind in the cane rushed to erase
> What they had to say. (Ménard, 285)

If in the first part the wind only listens, this time it quickly erases the men's conversation. The expression *"kouri efase"* suggests that there is an urgency and a conscious effort by the wind to get rid of the message. It seems like even mother nature does not want such bad news to be spread in order to avoid gossip.

The fifth part, which serves as the conclusion, reveals the truth that the husband might not have expected to hear. The *vyewo* returns from Haiti with a message from the wife: It is time for her husband to come back home:

> *Kouzen M' sot fè tè Ayiti*
> *Men youn komisyon, madanm ou voye ba-ou*
> *Kouzen li lè pou ou tounen*
> *Kouzen, menm si ou pa pot anyen*
> *Lè w'ap janbe fwontyè*
> *Pa bliye manchèt ou dèyè*

> Cousin, I come from working the land in Haiti.
> Here's a message your wife sent to you
> Cousin, she says it's time for you to return.
> Cousin, even if you have nothing to bring,
> When you cross the border,
> Don't leave your machete behind. (Ménard, 285)

The expression *"kouzen, menm si ou pa pot anyen"* suggests that he can come home as he is. His presence is more important than riches. The only tool he needs for the return is his machete: *"Pa bliye manchèt ou dèyè."* In this song, the word *"kouzen"* is used three times to show closeness, but also to get the attention of the friend the *vyewo* is trying to convince to go back home. Among Haitians, *cousin* is a term used to designate a comrade or friend, not necessarily a relative. This stanza gives the reader insights into the wife's thought process. She is a person who takes the time to analyze the situation facing her family and concludes that the best thing for the family would be for her husband to return home.[35] She kindly requests that the husband come back even if he does not bring anything[36] with him. She understands that coming from abroad is a burden on her husband. The expectation from the community is too high; anyone coming home from a foreign country is expected to look good, to be well-dressed, and to bring money to help family and friends. So, the wife anticipates people's reactions to her husband's shameful return but concludes that his presence is more important than negative public comments. The mention of the machete is significant. It is a tool[37] for a potential source of income that can also be used in Haiti to provide for the family. Returning with the machete means returning home to work the land. She is a wise woman capable of understanding the meaning of a broken home, the importance of rearing children together[38], and the strength of a nuclear family. The incredible actions of the wife illustrate well the famous saying in the Haitian community: *"fanm se poto mitan"* which means that women are the pillars of society. She manages to run the household daily and finds a way to meet her family's needs against the odds.

Conclusion

Although many songwriters tend to focus on the mistreatment of Haitians by the Dominican government and their harsh conditions in the bateyes, Martineau takes a different path, instead insisting on the heavy cross that wives bear in the absence of their husbands. In a subtle way, he shows the psychological impact of such a difficult situation on children, families, and relationships. By doing so, he adds another dimension to the debate about Haitian migration to the Dominican Republic. Yes, some Haitians believe that going to the Dominican Republic might improve their economic situation, but is it worth the pain and suffering endured by the ones left behind? The song clearly demonstrates that the money that the husband was able to send to his wife was so small that even the wife advises him to come back home. This song is the author's way of participating in the debate regarding Haitian migration to the Dominican Republic as well as a message to Haitians working in the bateyes to carefully evaluate their conditions. It is a song designed to be heard on the radio, which is the most important means of communication in Haiti. Martineau's linguistic choice is political because it reflects his national, cultural identity. By using Haitian Creole, he makes his work available to all Haitians.

Notes

1. Eddy Toussaint (Tontongi), in his article *"Jean-Claude Martineau an vedèt nan 'Livres en folie'*,*"* mentions that Jean-Claude Martineau has been praised by many of the most influential Haitian singers such as Carole Demesmin, Beethova Obas, Farah Juste, Emmeline Michel, and Manno Charlemagne among others. <http://www.tanbou.com/2021/JC-Martineau-Livres-en-follie.htm>
2. Foudou, Jean Numa. *"J. C Martineau, né avec la 'musique dans la tête'"*. Intexto. 19 octobre 2018. <https://www.intexto.ca/j-c-martineau-ne-avec-la-musique-dans-la-tete/>
3. For more information, see Félix Morisseau-Leroy's article "La littérature haïtienne d'expression créole Son avenir." Présence Africaine. N° 17, décembre 1957–janvier 1958, p. 47.
4. In the 1960s, Jean-Claude Martineau acquired the nickname Koralen, the Creole word for dugout canoe. He is now living in Montreal where he works as a writer, lyricist and radio commentator. For more information, see *"Les dimanches du conte. Nouveaux visages du conte au Québec."* <https://www.dimanchesduconte.com/archives/tag/jean-claude-martineau>
5. In an interview with Eddy Toussaint, Martineau provided some of the reasons why he left Haiti. Among them figured the absence of resources, an uncertain future, and the repressive political climate. Toussaint, Eddy. "Entèvyou ak Tonton Guy ak Jean-Claude Martineau." *Nouvelle stratégie*, Juillet 1985.
6. Statler Luczama: "Fanatique de la liberté d'expression, il rejoint les mouvements contre le régime dictatorial à la fin des années soixante, et va devoir laisser sa terre natale, en conséquence, pour s'installer aux États-Unis. Nostalgique, il trouve alors un refuge incommensurable dans le théâtre, l'écriture et la musique, qui finiront par se synchroniser dans son patrimoine artistique."
   Luczama, Statler. "Jean-Claude Martineau, une légende vivante dans la culture haïtienne." Le Quotidien. 29 janvier 2023. <https://lequotidiennews.org/jean-claude-martineau-une-legende-vivante-dans-la-culture-haitienne/>
7. The scholar Alain Sauval mentions that: "His talents as a storyteller, lyricist-composer, playwright and historian make him one of the greats of contemporary Haitian musical and literary creation."[1] Alain Sauval : "Ses talents de conteur, de parolier-compositeur, de dramaturge et d'historien en font l'un des grands de la création musicale et littéraire haïtienne contemporaine." Sauval, Alain. "Les contes de Jean-Claude Martineau ." Université Quisqueya. <https://uniq.edu.ht/les-contes-de-jean-claude-martineau/>
8. Martineau, Jean-Claude. Interview with Wedsly Turenne Guerrier. November 25, 2023.
9. Martineau, Jean-Claude. "Koze avèk Lodyans-Jean-Claude Martineau." Interview with Fred Williams. Komite Avansman Lang Kreyòl. 2022 <https://www.youtube.com/watch?v=we-nX_R53kA>

10. Martineau, Jean-Claude. "Entre nous: Jean-Claude Martineau (Koralen2)." Interview with Monique Lafontant. Radio Haiti Inter. March 10, 1991. <https://repository.duke.edu/dc/radiohaiti/RL10059-CS-1264_02>
11. Martineau, Jean-Claude. Interview with Wedsly Turenne Guerrier. November 25, 2023.
12. Ibid.
13. Legros Georges, Danielle. "Jean-Claude Martineau: Poet of the Underdog." *Consequence Forum*. 2022. <https://www.consequenceforum.org/translations/jean-claude-martineau-poet-of-the-underdog>
14. United States Institute of Peace.
15. Maguire, Robert. "Toward the End of Poverty in Haiti." United States Institute of Peace. December 1, 2008. <https://www.usip.org/publications/2008/12/toward-end-poverty-haiti>
16. Arthur, Charles and Dash, Michael. *A Haiti Anthology: Libète*. Markus Wiener Publishers, 1999.
17. Legros Georges, Danielle. "Jean-Claude Martineau: Poet of the Underdog." *Consequence Forum*. 2022. <https://www.consequenceforum.org/translations/jean-claude-martineau-poet-of-the-underdog>
18. Ibid.
19. Cassava has some properties that can fight cancer.
20. Martineau, Jean-Claude. "Face à l'Opinion: Koralen, Jean-Claude Martineau." Interview with Jean Dominique. April 15, 1997. <https://repository.duke.edu/dc/radiohaiti/RL10059-CS-0431_01>
21. Ibid.
22. Ibid.
23. Ibid.
24. Martineau, Jean-Claude. Interview with Wedsly Turenne Guerrier. November 25, 2023.
25. Ferguson, James. *Papa Doc, Baby Doc: Haiti and the Duvaliers*. B. Blackwell, 1987.
26. Talking about his book *Flè Dizè: Powèm Chante*, Martineau mentions, "What I want to convey is that we need a government that is responsive to the people's need. We need to develop our country and make it a place where Haitians are happy to live. This is my message. We can do a lot better than that." Martineau, Jean-Claude. Interview with Wedsly Turenne Guerrier. November 25, 2023.
27. Talking about "*Vyewo*," Martineau admits: "The refrain in that song is not from me. I heard it from my father, who had a lot of intellectual friends who would come to the house to chat. My mother would prepare dinner for them. I don't know if my father created that song, if it came from the group that he was in, or if they created it together. I just build the rest of the song on that refrain. I completed the song because of the situation in Haiti and also because it was an homage to my father. I composed the whole song on a few sentences that I heard my father sing. Not only the words, but also the music he used to sing with it. And it stuck in my mind, and I completed it." Ibid.
28. Working in a batey, a sugar cane field, is not an easy task: the sun is hot; the sugarcane leaves can cut the skin and cause bleeding that can lead to infections if not properly treated. Any mistake made by the cane cutter with the machete can result in finger cuts or serious injuries. The workers know how dangerous such a job can be, but they sacrifice their lives in an attempt to provide for their families.

29   The first six lines serve as a refrain to the song as they are repeated in the third strophe. In this song, there are flat and crossed rhymes. The first stanza rhyme ABABCBCBBDEECD. The second strophe rhyme DDBCBDCCFF. The third strophe rhyme ABABCBCBBDDGG.
30   In discussing the poem, the scholar Nadève Ménard notes that: "Although its references to space are specific, it remains vague in terms of time, giving the impression that it could be describing a scene from the past or a reality that is very much current." (Ménard, 284).
      Ménard, Nadève. *The Haiti reader: History, Culture, Politics.* Duke University Press, 2020.
31   Ménard, Nadève. *The Haiti reader: History, Culture, Politics.* Duke University Press, 2020.
32   The mention of *"manman"* shows that the man has a deep relationship with his mother, but his wife is his priority.
33   The husband, by sending the friend to spy on his wife and possibly give his mother what was destined for his wife in case of infidelity, displays the type of power he can exercise over her, putting her in a disadvantaged position.
34   In Haitian Creole the word *plasaj* means "Common law marriage, concubinage. It is a system whereby a man shacks up with a woman or different women (whether he be married or not) and they live as man and wife, without the benefit of clergy." Jean Targète and Raphael G. Urciolo. *Haitian Creole-English Dictionary. Haitian Creole-English Dictionary.* <https://www.hopeforhaitischildren.org/hfhcmedia/Haitian_Creole_English_Dictionary_2nd_printing.pdf>
35   The wife, by pointing out the lack of prosperity from the husband and his absence in the family, has the authority to legitimize her request for her husband to return home.
36   The critics Gerard Leavy and Johanne Eliacin mention that "The 'disappointment' theory, for example, purports that immigrants return home because they have failed to achieve their goals for migration." (p. 204). This is clearly the case in "Vyewo."
      Leavy, Gerard and Eliacin, Johanne. "The Past is a foreign country: vulnerability to mental illness among return migrants." *Return Migration in Later Life: International Perspective.* Edited by John Percival. Policy Press, 2013.
37   It is worth mentioning that the "machete" is also the weapon used by Dominicans to kill thousands of Haitians during the Haitian Massacre. In 1937, the Dominican President Rafael Trujillo ordered the massacre of Haitians in the Dominican Republic. Trujillo launched a campaign against what Michael Kimmelman called a "silent invasion" in his article "Germany's new 'textbook' on the Holocaust" (2008). According to the critic Eric Paul Roorda, "Although estimates of the duration of the massacre and its Death toll vary widely, it seems likely that 12,000 Haitians died during at least a week of violence throughout the country." Some other estimates run between 15, 0000 and 30,000 Haitian victims.
      Kimmelman, Michael. "Germany's new 'textbook' on the Holocaust." *The New York Times.* 27 Feb. 2008.
      Roorda, Eric Paul. "Genocide Next Door: The Good Neighbor Policy, the Trujillo Regime, and the Haitian Massacre of 1937." *Diplomatic History,* Summer 1996, Vol 20, No. 3 (Summer 1996), pp. 301–319.
38   It is worth noting that in the absence of her husband, the wife is expected to do everything, have the entire family on her shoulders, which includes, among other things, raising children, providing food and shelter, sending them to school if possible, taking care of older parents etc.

Bibliography

Arthur, Charles and Dash, Michael. *A Haiti Anthology: Libète.* Markus Wiener Publishers, 1999.

Ferguson, James. *Papa Doc, Baby Doc: Haiti and the Duvaliers.* B. Blackwell, 1987.

Foudou, Jean Numa. "J. C Martineau, né avec la 'musique dans la tête'." *Intexto.* 19 octobre 2018. <https://www.intexto.ca/j-c-martineau-ne-avec-la-musique-dans-la-tete/>

Kimmelman, Michael. "Germany's new 'textbook' on the Holocaust." The New York Times. 27 Feb. 2008.

Leavy, Gerard and Eliacin, Johanne. "The Past is a foreign country": vulnerability to mental illness among return migrants. *Return Migration in Later Life: International Perspective.* Edited by John Percival. Policy Press, 2013.

Legros Georges, Danielle. "Jean-Claude Martineau: Poet of the Underdog." *Consequence Forum.* 2022. <https://www.consequenceforum.org/translations/jean-claude-martineau-poet-of-the-underdog>

Luczama, Statler. "Jean-Claude Martineau, une légende vivante dans la culture haïtienne." *Le Quotidien.* 29 janvier 2023. <https://lequotidiennews.org/jean-claude-martineau-une-legende-vivante-dans-la-culture-haitienne/>

Maguire, Robert. "Toward the End of Poverty in Haiti." *United States Institute of Peace.* December 1, 2008. <https://www.usip.org/publications/2008/12/toward-end-poverty-haiti>

Martineau, Jean-Claude. "Entre nous: Jean-Claude Martineau (Koralen2)." *Radio Haiti Inter.* March 10, 1991. <https://repository.duke.edu/dc/radiohaiti/RL10059-CS-1264_02>

———. Interview with Wedsly Turenne Guerrier. November 25, 2023.

———. *Flè Dizè : Powèm chante.* Marika Roumain, 1982.

———. "Koze avèk Lodyans-Jean-Claude Martineau." Interview with Fred Williams. *Komite Avansman Lang Kreyòl.* 2022. <https://www.youtube.com/watch?v=we-nX_R53kA>

Ménard, Nadève. *The Haiti reader: History, Culture, Politics.* Duke University Press, 2020.

Morisseau-Leroy, Félix. "La littérature haïtienne d'expression créole Son avenir." *Présence Africaine.* N° 17, décembre 1957–janvier 1958, p. 47.

Roorda, Eric Paul. "Genocide Next Door: The Good Neighbor Policy, the Trujillo Regime, and the Haitian Massacre of 1937." *Diplomatic History,* Summer 1996, Vol 20, No. 3 (Summer 1996), pp. 301–319.

Sauval, Alain. "Les contes de Jean-Claude Martineau." *Université Quisqueya*. <https://uniq.edu.ht/les-contes-de-jean-claude-martineau/>

Targète, Jean and Urciolo, Raphael G. *Haitian Creole-English Dictionary. Haitian Creole-English Dictionary*. <https://www.hopeforhaitischildren.org/hfhcmedia/Haitian_Creole_English_Dictionary_2nd_printing.pdf>

Toussaint, Eddy. "Entèvyou ak Tonton Guy ak Jean-Claude Martineau." *Nouvelle stratégie*, Juillet 1985.

———. "Jean-Claude Martineau an vedèt nan 'Livres en folie'." June 10, 2021. <http://www.tanbou.com/2021/JC-Martineau-Livres-en-follie.htm>

Time for Action: "*Manman, pa ban m tete ankò*" (Mother, stop breastfeeding me)

Introduction

Although Haitian Creole is "the medium in which Haitian independence was conceived and best expressed"[1] (Lang 128), it has long been a subject of controversy. After 1804, The Haitian government and elite saw it as a language that should be used in only informal settings. The renowned Martinican psychiatrist Frantz Fanon[2] was one of the first critics to observe that: "In the French Antilles the bourgeoisie does not use Creole except when speaking to servants. At school the young Martinican is taught to treat the dialect with contempt. Avoid Creolisms. Some families forbid speaking Creole at home, and mothers call their children little ragamuffins for using it."[3] (4) Therefore, in order to see Haitian Creole enjoy a perceived higher and more comprehensive social status, many Haitian scholars took the initiative to promote it as the language that could express the heart and soul of the Haitian people.[4] Emmanuel W. Védrine, a Haitian linguist, poet, essayist, and educator, has worked tirelessly in that regard. In the 1990s, he became aware of the lack of books available in that language and decided to research and publish in Creole. His 700-page Bibliography on Haitian Creole was published in 2003. The linguist Albert Valdmann was "impressed with Védrine's motivation for the Development of Haitian Creole as a language that can be standardized and adapted to serve all the functions of its speakers, and, in particular, members of the Diaspora who required medical, social, and educational services in the language."[5] This chapter is an analysis of one of Védrine's poems: *"Manman, pa banm tete ankò"* ("Mother, stop breastfeeding me"). I argue that beyond its obvious meaning, this poem can also be interpreted as the appeal of the Haitian people to those who thwart their independence.

CHAPTER 6

Biography of Emmanuel W. Védrine

Emmanuel W. Védrine was born in *L'Asile* (Haiti) on January 15, 1959. In discussing his hometown, Védrine boasts that:

> I grew up in an environment called *Lazil* (Jerémie) which was like paradise. When I opened my window, I saw the most beautiful mountains, guinea fowls that were flying, and many animals that were flying. There are three rivers for example that become one. When you arrived at the front door of our house, we stayed on a hill, you could hear the sound of that river. When you got down to the bottom of this valley, when you spoke you could hear the echo for example. So, I grew up in a poetic environment.[6]

During his childhood, Védrine read many books because there were plenty of them in his house. The books that he had at his disposal coupled with the majestic environment in which he grew up inspired him to become a writer. In 1976, he moved to the United States to join his parents. Védrine studied at the university level in both the United States and Europe. He earned bachelor's degrees in different disciplines such as Romance Languages, Education, General linguistics and Social Sciences. He also earned graduate degrees in Bilingual Education (University of Massachusetts), French and Creole Linguistics (Indiana University), Theoretical Linguistics (Harvard University). Védrine is a polyglot. A certified teacher of French and Spanish in Massachusetts, he can also speak Creole, English, German, Italian, and Papiamento. He has taught in High School as well as in several Universities such as The Boston Language Institute, The University of Rhode Island, and Indiana University. He wrote more than 70 articles, several essays, and multiple books. He has been writing about topics such as language, politics, and reforestation for 31 years. In his capacity as an activist, he provides training sessions in various disciplines, for young people, politicians, and Church members. His seminars and conferences are available on YouTube.

Emmanuel W. Védrine has a unique experience with Haitian Creole and Education. He started teaching in 1986 in the Haitian bilingual program in Boston. At that time, the dictatorial government of President Jean-Claude Duvalier was uprooted and many Haitians were leaving Haiti. Among them were a lot of young students who came from different school levels / grades. Therefore, the majority of such students attending the Boston public school did not have an advanced level of education in Haiti. A short number of them got to middle school or High School. However, many of them did not have a solid education in order to make the transition in Boston. Those students had not only to learn English quickly in the Bilingual program, because the bilingual program gave them three years to learn English, after they could start the mainstream as they call it in English. Once the students got to mainstream, all the courses they were in English. Therefore, they were no longer exposed to Haitian instructors. So, whichever course they were teaching, some instructors were teaching math, some were teaching sciences, they explained everything in the students' language which is Creole, but all the books were in English. Such an experience helped Védrine to understand the linguistic issue in Haiti. As he mentioned during my interview with him:

> Not only was I working to summarize what I was doing in English, I was also explaining it in Creole. That is how I witnessed the students' shortcomings. I saw the big problems that existed in Haiti's schools. In order to better serve the students, I had to interview them, asking how long they had been in school in Haiti, what grade they arrived at, what type of school they were in. Some of them came from the provinces / country sides. We were dealing with all these problems in the bilingual school. It was quite a laboratory for me as someone who was teaching U.S history, world history, social studies, and how to guide the children to their careers.[7]

Studying linguistics plays a key role in shaping Védrine's thought process. He admits that:

> When you study linguistics, there is a mental evolution that takes place inside of you. When you study linguistics, you learn to appreciate the mother tongue and they don't teach us to appreciate it in Haiti. They teach us to reject everything that belongs to us in Haiti. So, it's a kind of colonial education that we receive. And one of the ingredients that is very specific to you that you are taught to reject is Creole.[8]

Védrine stresses that linguistics makes one appreciate the mother tongue and its importance. According to him, the mother tongue is like a genetic code, it is part of one's blood. Linguistics makes you see the mother tongue's importance in education so that you can value it in everything. He ties linguistics to a psychological revolution that prompts people to appreciate their mother tongue. In discussing the linguistics situation in Haiti, he admits that

> We [Haitians] do not grow up in an environment where we hear everybody speaking French. No, it's a Creole environment where we all speak Creole. No matter where you go in Haiti, you see, you have no problem speaking Creole. You see that it's not a French environment, it's not a Francophone environment, it's a Creolophone environment.[9]

Aware of the linguistics issue in Haiti and the weakness of the Haitian students who were attending the Bilingual school in Boston, Védrine took the initiative to help out by producing Haitian Creole materials and making them available online. He is an author who has written about many issues and used different genres. He edited many literary works. His works have been published in anthologies, journals, magazines, publishing houses, and the web. Védrine admits that

CHAPTER 6

writing in Haitian Creole was not an easy task for him because some people tried to discourage him:

> When I began working and writing, I was told that there was no market in Creole. I was asked "why do it if no one was going to read it?" But my work has never been about marketing. I want to do something to help Haiti-money does not come first. Knowing that thousands benefit from my work makes me happy. Forget about the market, I just want to do something that will change lives.[10] (Quoted in Louis)

The scholar Martine Louis, in her article "Védrine committed to bridging the language gap" mentioned that "While teaching in Massachusetts, Védrine discovered that many of his Haitian students were falling behind academically and noted that learning material in their native language would improve the quality of their education. In 1992, he published his first *Dictionary of Haitian Creole verbs with phrases and idioms*."[11] Emmanuel Védrine often talks about some of the barriers that Haitian Creole has to surmount in order to be used as a language that can be utilized to identify and solve Haitian problems. He emphasizes that the Haitian government has to play a greater role in implementing Creole in its administration and in schools: "The Haitian government removed the Creole language from many of their documents. If you go to the government website, for example Haitian consulates, everything is in French. They are not all translated into Creole."[12] He believes that in Haitian schools, teaching must be done in Creole in Haiti. He sees Haitian Creole not only as means of communication, but also as a tool that can be used toward the Development of the nation. He stresses that some Haitians should get rid of the colonial mentality that prevents them from embracing Creole as the language of instruction in school. Like Jean-Claude Martineau, Védrine believes that: "We come from a time that has taught us to hate ourselves and what we own. We have been taught to leave our country behind and move on to a 'better' place. This is why Haiti is consistently suffering crisis after crisis. We need a 'new school'. One that will teach us to be proud of our roots."[13] (Quoted in Louis).

In 1992, driven by the desire to make a positive impact in the Haitian community, Védrine launched the E. W. Védrine Creole Project which has been running for 31 years. The purpose of this project was to develop teaching materials for Haitian Bilingual Programs in Haiti as well as the United States and for learners of Haitian Creole. He invested his own money so that people could access these materials free of charge. When I asked him why he embarked on such an endeavor, he stated the following:

> I want to raise a challenge to show Haitians that it is not money that prevents us from doing great things in Haiti, but our mentality. It's one of the messages I want to give

with my project where I use my own money to do all these jobs without asking for a grant. Don't forget I live in the USA. I could go and ask for grants right and left. No. I'm not doing it because I want to show Haitians that there are extraordinary things we can do with Haiti, but it's our mentality that blocks us.[14]

With the support of his family and using his own salary, he has been able to pay for the costs associated with his project. He subscribes to the notion that the Haitian mentality has to change in order to bring real change in Haiti: "We must dream high."[15] He believes that Haitians should ask for information, stay united, and involve the Haitian diaspora to participate in the changes that Haiti needs. He stresses that many people in the diaspora have money, connections, and human resources to help bring changes to Haiti. The problem is they do not work in concert with the people of Haiti. In discussing his legacy, Védrine mentions that "The biggest thing I have accomplished as a writer is that my 30 years of work are made available free of charge to the Haitian people."[16]

His historical novel *Sezon sechrès Ayiti: Woman ayisyen*[17], published in 1994, tackles Haiti's ecological problem. In this book, he laments the fact that Haiti suffers a severe problem of drought, deforestation and erosion caused by peasants' cutting down too many trees for charcoal. He argues that if the government provided electricity to the people, they would not have resorted to using charcoal to prepare their meals. In his essay "Haiti and the destruction of nature"[18], Védrine underlines that in order to bring real change in Haiti:

> Agricultural Development should be a #1 priority for advancement of Haiti's prospects. Haitian peasants need land to work, they need water to irrigate their plots of land, they need to grow whatever they can eat and to support their family, using money from the sale of their excess produce to purchase other necessities of life. To conclude, developing agriculture throughout Haiti would be one of the best answers to stop Haitian peasants from crossing the border to the Dominican Republic (illegally or legally; thereby supporting the Black market behind this trade) and would be one of the most important steps in changing Haiti's face."[19]

Védrine is an author who is always looking for ways to help Haitians reflect on their living conditions and find ways to improve themselves. The poem analyzed below is part of this strategy.

"Manman, pa ban m tete ankò"

"*Manman, pa ban m tete ankò*" "Mother stop breastfeeding me" is a poem[20] that depicts the complicated relationship between a mother and her child. Although it is made of a single stanza, it can be divided into four parts; each

CHAPTER 6

one brings another dimension to the narrator's argument. There are only two exclamation points and a period in the poem. The lack of punctuation signals the flow of the poem as well as its sense of urgency. The title, which identifies the addressee as the mother, is a firm expression of a child who no longer needs to be breastfed. The negative expression *"pa ... ankò"* clearly expresses the narrator's desire not to be breastfed anymore. The short, brief lines used throughout the poem give it a sense of urgency, underlining a confrontation. From the start, the child narrator positions himself as the person in command-no longer a passive, dependent infant, he is a revolutionary standing up for himself:

Li lè pou sevre m
Mwen fè dan
Mwen ka mòde ou

It is time to wean me
I have teeth
I can bite you

In the first part of the poem, the narrator declares that he is tired of drinking his mother's milk. His insistence on the notion of time suggests that he has been waiting for a while, but he is now ready for a drastic change. The expression *"li lè"* expresses the narrator's impatience toward his mother. Not only can't he wait any longer, but he also identifies his natural weapons that can be used to cause harm to his mother in order to get her attention. The pronoun *"m,"* which is the contraction of *"mwen,"* underlines that the narrator is talking about a personal issue dear to his heart. The words: *"fè dan"* and *"ka mòde"* show what he is capable of doing to her.

Many experts insist that breastfeeding is crucial to children's healthy growth and Development. For instance, Colin Binns, MiKyung Lee and Wah Yun Low in their article entitled "The Long-term Benefits of Breastfeeding" provide a compelling argument in favor of this.[21] What is interesting about the child in the poem is that he understands that the time for breastfeeding for him should be over. In his request to his mother, he does not deny the importance of breastfeeding. He simply suggests that for a child his age, mother's milk is not enough to keep him strong.

In the second part of the poem, the narrator provides a general idea of the type of food he is requesting:

Tanpri souple
Ban m bon jan manje
Pou m manje

Mwen bezwen bon jan
Vitamin pou m kanpe

Please
Give me adequate food
To eat
I need appropriate
Vitamins to be strong

It is worth noting that the phrase "Tanpri souple" shows a sign of respect toward the mother. The word "manje" is mentioned twice to emphasize that he is asking for solid food, not liquid. The assonance or repetition of the nasal vowels "an" (bright and open sound) in the line "Ban m bonjan manje" expresses the anger of the narrator. He enumerates the type of food he considers adequate for a child his age that the mother should provide him. The turn of phrase "Ban m" explains what the mother should give him and "Mwen bezwen" reinforces his demand. Likewise, the expression "bon jan" says something about the quality of food that he is requesting. It underlines the nutritive quality as well as the sizable portion needed. It is apparent that vitamins are of great importance to the narrator in order to be able to fight diseases and hunger. The verb "kanpe" implies the idea of being strong and capable of fighting diseases.

This precocious child is aware of his condition. He enumerates all the foods he has been given, but that are not appropriate for him:

Pap ban m ti jèbè
Ak ti labouyi nan kiyè!
Pap ban m bwè nan bibon
Mwen pa ti bebe
Pa pran m pou egare!

Don't give me small Gerber
And small porridge in spoons
Don't feed me in bottles
I am not a little baby
Don't think that I am stupid!

If in the second part of the poem, the narrator spoke about what he should receive, in this third part, he mentions what his mother should not offer him as food anymore. The negative expression "pa," is used three times to emphasize such an idea. Likewise, the adjective "ti," stresses the pettiness of the food that he no longer wants to see near him. This idea is illustrated through words such as "ti jèbè," "ti kiyè," and "bibon." Gerber is a type of baby food produced in the United States: The Gerber baby is an advertising icon from the Gerber Product

Company. The last two lines display his ability to reason with his mother by presenting solid arguments to back up his claim. The repetition of the high-pitched sound "i" in the line "Ak ti labouyi nan ti kiyè" underlines the shout of the narrator while expressing himself. The repetition of the hard consonant "p" in the line "pa pran m pou egare" gives a sense of abruptness or authority. He insinuates that he is not an intellectually challenged or a confused dummy. He is depicted as knowing what is good for a child his age:

> Manman, tanpri souple
> Pa kontinye
> Ban m tete
> M wè lèt ou sale
> Li ka ban m vant pase
> Kite m bwè lèt bouyi
> Pap ban m ti labouyi
> Ou konnen m pa timoun piti
> Manman, pa ban m tete
> Mwen kòmanse pale.

> Mother, please
> Stop
> Breastfeeding me
> I find your milk to be salty
> It can give me an upset stomach
> Let me drink boiled milk
> Stop giving me small porridge
> You know that I am not a small baby
> Mother, stop breastfeeding me
> I start to talk

In the first line of the fourth part of the poem, one notices the expression of supplication used by the narrator to talk to his mother: "*Manman, tanpri souple.*" He seems to take all sorts of precautions so that the situation does not degenerate. In this section, he continues his argument to prove his point. For example, "*M wè lèt ou sale*" means that such salty milk cuts his appetite. Since he is not going to drink it, he will be starving. He goes even further by saying: "*Li ka ban m vant pase*" which suggests that his mother's milk can cause his indigestion. The expression "*kite m bwè lèt bouyi*" suggests that the narrator witnesses boiled[22] milk around the house, but it is the mother who prevents him from drinking such milk. He reiterates again his aversion toward "*ti labouyi.*" The expression "*m pa timoun piti*" implies that he is an intelligent human-being who is capable of understanding what is good for him, and no one can take that away from him. He understands the ruse of his mother to feed him baby food that can only keep him in a childish state. He has ample knowledge and many weapons at his disposal to make his voice heard. The expression "*Mwen kòmanse pale*" suggests that he is able to express his true feelings, make his demands, and spread the news around. He knows that he will use his words as needed to stand up for himself.

Many people have stories about how mothers want to raise their children and what they want them to eat. This poem, however, offers the child's point of view about nutrition. People who think that children are sometimes too young to discuss certain issues might be surprised to see how intelligent this child is. He is old enough to see that his mother's salty milk is not good for his digestion. What he wants is boiled milk—the purified kind, maybe the expensive one full of vitamins good for older children. The author denounces infantilization. That means the mother thinks that the child does not grow, cannot care for himself, and cannot make big decisions.

What works in the child's favor is his ability to speak out against what he considers to be abusive. He recognizes that he has two weapons at his disposal and has the courage to use them appropriately: first, his teeth can cause his mother pain. Frantz Fanon, in *The Wretched of the Earth* reminds us that sometimes in order to be heard, we have to use force, violence. This child is well aware of his capability and is ready to fight. The second weapon is speech, his ability to express his concerns. He lets his mother know that he understands the game; the time to suffer in silence is over and it is time to finally get what he deserves. By introducing the subaltern voice into the discourse, the child challenges the mother in what she believes she does best. By doing so, he opens the way for people everywhere, who are victims of neglectful benevolence.

According to Roland Barthes[23] (1915–1980), readers hold in their hands all possible meanings of the text, which implies that there are many ways to interpret this poem. It can be seen as a simple work that talks about tensions between a child and his mother. Alternatively, one can argue that the mother can symbolize anyone in a position of power: a boss, a partner, an NGO, a government, a colonial power, etc. Since the author is Haitian, the poem can be read as a national or international allegory if we interpret the child in the poem as Haitian, the mother as an NGO, and the MINUSTAH (UN Security Forces) represents a colonial power or an international force. In that sense, the poem suggests that Haiti no longer needs superficial help: to stand on its feet and grow, it needs resources that can help it to be strong against adversity. It needs economic and political independence in order to grow as a true nation. It cannot be treated like a child who keeps receiving baby food. It wants freedom to make its own decisions and develop as other autonomous nations do.

CHAPTER 6

Although written in the 1990s, this poem is relevant to the current times. For example, after the devastating earthquake in 2010, many Haitians felt that the international community treated their country as a child. The scholar Shearon Roberts argues that:

> To date, Haiti has the highest number of nongovernmental agencies per capita in the world, with foreign NGOs conducting Haiti's reconstruction independently of the Haitian government. As of 2015, the Haitian government receives less than 10 percent of the international aid set aside to sustainably rebuild Haiti, and over 90 percent of the NGOs receiving foreign aid for projects in Haiti are non-Haitian entities who do not coordinate with Haitian government ministries or need to answer to the Haitian government or its people. The reconstruction Development aid through US-led UN-coordinated Haiti Reconstruction Fund undermined Haiti's political institutions, proposed unsustainable economic models for Haiti, and marginalized ordinary Haitians, primarily by denying them a say in the country's future.[24] (Roberts, 242)

That is why, like the child in the poem, Haitian scholars such as Gina Athena Ulysse[25], Isabel MacDonald[26], Evelyne Trouillot[27], and Alex Dupuy[28] stood up to reiterate that Haiti's agenda should be set by the Haitian people. They acknowledge that the international community can help to implement it. Foreign companies can offer their expertise upon request to help articulate solutions based on Haitian reality. Many scholars like Mark Sculler and Pablo Morales,[29] Beverly Bell[30], Mark Weisbrot[31] expressed that bringing profound improvement to the lives of the Haitian people requires more than just the repair and reconstruction of homes damaged during the 2010 earthquake—infrastructure must be rebuilt. Effective building codes and zoning laws must be formulated and enforced, and an organized land-titling system must be created and utilized if changes made in the housing sector are to be truly sustainable. Long-term progress will be ensured only if the capacity of the Haitian government is strengthened, addressing the underlying issue behind many of Haiti's Development challenges. The presence of the UN Security forces in Haiti and the interference of the OAS in Haiti's presidential elections are barriers—unwanted breast milk—to Haiti's growth.

When I asked Védrine to comment about his poem "*Manman pa ban m tete ankò*," he argued that

> This poem has to do with colonization. It is a rhetorical figure. It has to do with any country, for example, that is oppressing Haiti. So, these colonizing countries, they don't teach you anything, but they make it seem like they are helping you. They keep you at a childish level so that you will never evolve. When you start to become aware of these colonizing countries, you have a feeling of revolt when you consider their abuse toward you.[32]

Védrine's poem is relevant on an international scale these days because we see for example what is happening in Africa. A series of countries (Mali, Burkina Faso, Niger) that France colonized and exploited stood up to reclaim their sovereignty. We also see the awakening that is taking place in Haiti. In October 2023, the peasants of Ouanaminthe[33] took matters into their own hands by digging the canal that will help them irrigate the Maribaroux Plain that can produce tons of food for their survival. They had been waiting for years for the Haitian government to act on their behalf, when they saw no follow-up, and a drought was causing too many problems with their crops, they stood up for their rights and dug the canal themselves with the help of the Haitian diaspora. Many Haitians see this movement as a revolution, a psychological awakening in the Haitian mentality. Water is very important for agriculture, for reforestation, it is important for animals. Talking about the canal movement, Védrine suggests the following:

> Let's have canals everywhere in all communes of Haiti in order to have plenty of food to eat and everything else that needs to be done, free schools because we don't have free schools. You can't talk about Development without free schooling for children up to High school. It is impossible. We need ports, we need airports, we need roads, we need incoming tourists. All this is the channel of Development we need.[34]

Conclusion

In conclusion, it can be argued that Védrine uses this poem to awaken Haitian consciousness. The poem seems to suggest that if a child can stand up for himself, anyone should be able to do the same. What is interesting in this poem is that the mother has no chance or opportunity to respond to the narrator's demand. Since the poem is just one stanza, the poet uses perhaps such a form to emphasize the point of view of the narrator and provides him with a platform to express himself without any interruption.

This short poem that appears to be about tensions between a mother and her child is an allegory that can be interpreted in different ways. Since it was written by a Haitian author, it can symbolize the cry of the Haitian people against the negative impact of the international community in Haiti's Development. Under the pretext of providing humanitarian help to Haiti, the international community uses NGOs that ignore the Haitian government agencies, but they cannot solve Haiti's dire problems. These piece-meal solutions are designed to keep Haiti in an undeveloped state. This poem can be served as a model to help Haitians open their eyes to understand the tactics utilized by the former colonizers through international organizations. It is fair to say that the poem has an international

CHAPTER 6

tone to it because any former colonized country can be seen as the rebel child reclaiming real change. Likewise, the mother can be seen as anyone in a position of authority or power trying to manipulate other people, preventing them from spreading their wings. With his work, Emmanuel Védrine proves that the popular language, that had been despised for so long, is of great importance. It can be used to tackle serious issues.

Notes

1. Lang, George. "A Primer of Haitian Literature in 'Kreyòl.'" *Research in African Literatures*, vol. 35, no. 2, 2004, pp. 128–40. JSTOR, <http://www.jstor.org/stable/3821349>. Accessed 17 Nov. 2023.
2. Although his remarks apply to Martinican Creole, they are applicable to Haitian Creole as well.
3. Fanon, Frantz. *Black Skin, White Masks*. Translated by Markman Charles Lam. Grove Press, 1967.
4. The scholar Tony Jean-Jacques, in the introduction of Védrine's collection of poems called *Poetry in Haitian Creole: A guide for beginners and translators*, mentions the following about Védrine: "He follows his own road, believes in his own style, and pursues his own dreams, which are deeply rooted in the Haitian dream. He refuses to separate himself from the 'common Haitian.'" (p. 4)

    Védrine, Emmanuel W. *Poetry in Haitian Creole: A guide for beginners and translators*. Soup To Nuts Publishers, 1993.
5. <http://www.potomitan.info/vedrine/#18>
6. Védrine, Emmanuel W. Interview with Wedsly Turenne Guerrier. November 2, 2023.
7. Védrine, Emmanuel W. Interview with Wedsly Turenne Guerrier Ph.D. November 2, 2023.
8. Ibid.
9. Ibid.
10. Louis, Martine. "Védrine committed to bridging language gap." *Boston Haitian Reporter*. Vol 6, Issue 9, Sept 2007. <https://www.potomitan.info/vedrine/language.php#:~:text=%E2%80%9CVedrine%20committed%20to%20bridging%20language%20gap%E2%80%9D&text=Successful%20language%20scholar%20Emmanuel%20W,aspects%20of%20the%20Haitian%20culture>.
11. Ibid.
12. Védrine, Emmanuel W. Interview with Wedsly Turenne Guerrier. November 2, 2023.
13. Louis, Martine. "Védrine committed to bridging language gap." *Boston Haitian Reporter*. Vol 6, Issue 9, Sept 2007. <https://www.potomitan.info/vedrine/language.php#:~:text=%E2%80%9CVedrine%20committed%20to%20bridging%20language%20gap%E2%80%9D&text=Successful%20language%20scholar%20Emmanuel%20W,aspects%20of%20the%20Haitian%20culture>.
14. Védrine, Emmanuel W. Interview with Wedsly Turenne Guerrier. November 2, 2023.
15. Ibid.
16. Ibid.

17 Védrine, Emmanuel W. *Sezon sechrès Ayiti: Woman ayisyen*. Soup To Nuts Publishers, 1994.
18 This essay was originally written in Haitian Creole with this title "*Ayiti, yon peyi ravaje nou dwe sispann detwi*." It was published in *Bòn Nouvèl*, No. 352. June 1999.
19 Védrine, Emmanuel W. "Haiti and the Destruction of Nature." November 10, 2002. <http://www.hartford-hwp.com/archives/43a/254.html>.
20 The poem was published in the collection called *Poetry in Haitian Creole: A guide for beginners and translators* which was published by Soup To Nuts Publishers in 1993.
21 Binns, Colin, Lee, MiKyung, and Low, Wah Yun. "The Long-Term Benefits of Breastfeeding." *Asia Pacific Journal of Public Health*, Vol 28, No 1 (January 2016), pp. 7–14.
22 It is worth pointing out that in Haiti, when people buy cow milk, they usually boil it before consuming it. It is true that in most families, this type of milk is for grownups because children usually have their own kind already.
23 Barthes, Roland. "De l'œuvre au texte." *Le bruissement de la langue*, Paris: Seuil, 1984, pp. 69–77.
24 Roberts, Shearon. "Then and Now: Haitian Journalism as Resistance to U.S. Occupation and U.S.-Led Reconstruction." *Journal of Haitian Studies*. Fall 2015, Vol. 21, special Issue on the Us Occupation of Haiti, 1915–1934, pp. 241–268.
25 Ulysse, Gina Athena. *Why Haiti needs New Narratives Now More Than Ever: A Post-Quake Chronicle*. Wesleyan University Press, 2015.
26 MacDonald, Isabel and Doucet, Isabeau. "The Shelters that Clinton Built," *The Nation*, July 11, 2011.
27 Trouillot, Evelyne. "Abse sou Klou: Reconstructing Exclusion." In *Tectonic Shifts: Haiti Since the Earthquake*. Kumarian Press, 2012.
28 Dupuy, Alex. "Beyond the Earthquake: A Wake-Up Call for Haiti." *Latin American Perspectives*, vol. 37, no. 3, 2010, pp. 195–204.
29 Schuller, Mark and Morales, Pablo. *Tectonic Shifts: Haiti since the Earthquake*. Sterling, VA: Kumarian Press. Haitian Creole edition published 2013.
30 Bell, Beverly. "'We Bend, but We don't Break': Fighting for a just Reconstruction in Haiti." *Nacla*. July 8, 2010. <https://nacla.org/news/%E2%80%98we-bend-we-don%E2%80%99t-break%E2%80%99-fighting-just-reconstruction-haiti>.
31 Weisbrot, Mark. "Haiti and the International Aid Scam." The Guardian (UK), April 22, 2011.
32 Védrine, Emmanuel W. Interview with Wedsly Turenne Guerrier Ph.D. November 2, 2023.
33 *Ouanaminthe* is a commune or town located in the Nord-Est department of Haiti.
34 Védrine, Emmanuel W. Interview with Wedsly Turenne Guerrier Ph.D. November 2, 2023.

Bibliography

Barthes, Roland. "De l'œuvre au texte." *Le bruissement de la langue*, Paris: Seuil, 1984, pp. 69–77.

Bell, Beverly. "'We Bend, but We don't Break': Fighting for a just Reconstruction in Haiti." *Nacla*. July 8, 2010. <https://nacla.org/news/%E2%80%98we-bend-we-don%E2%80%99t-break%E2%80%99-fighting-just-reconstruction-haiti>

Binns, Colin, Lee, MiKyung and Low, Wah Yun. "The Long-Term Benefits of Breastfeeding." *Asia Pacific Journal of Public Health*, Vol 28, No 1 (January 2016), pp. 7–14.

Dupuy, Alex. "Beyond the Earthquake: A Wake-Up Call for Haiti." *Latin American Perspectives*, vol. 37, no. 3, 2010, pp. 195–204.

Fanon, Frantz. *Black Skin, White Masks*. Translated by Markman Charles Lam. Grove Press, 1967.

Lang, George. "A Primer of Haitian Literature in 'Kreyòl.'" *Research in African Literatures*, vol. 35, no. 2, 2004, pp. 128–40. JSTOR, <http://www.jstor.org/stable/3821349>. Accessed 17 Nov. 2023.

Louis, Martine. "Védrine committed to bridging language gap." *Boston Haitian Reporter*. Vol 6, Issue 9, Sept 2007. <https://www.potomitan.info/vedrine/language.php#:~:text=%E2%80%9CVedrine%20committed%20to%20bridging%20language%20gap%E2%80%9D&text=Successful%20language%20scholar%20Emmanuel%20W,aspects%20of%20the%20Haitian%20culture>.

MacDonald, Isabel and Doucet, Isabeau. "The Shelters that Clinton Built," *The Nation*, July 11, 2011.

Roberts, Shearon. "Then and Now: Haitian Journalism as Resistance to U.S. Occupation and US-Led Reconstruction." *Journal of Haitian Studies*. Fall 2015, Vol. 21, special Issue on the Us Occupation of Haiti, 1915–1934, pp. 241–268.

Schuller, Mark and Morales, Pablo. *Tectonic Shifts: Haiti since the Earthquake*. Sterling, VA: Kumarian Press. Haitian Creole edition published 2013.

Trouillot, Evelyne. "Abse sou Klou: Reconstructing Exclusion." In *Tectonic Shifts: Haiti Since the Earthquake*. Kumarian Press, 2012.

Ulysse, Gina Athena. *Why Haiti needs New Narratives Now More Than Ever: A Post-Quake \Chronicle*. Wesleyan University Press, 2015.

Védrine, Emmanuel W. "Haiti and the Destruction of Nature." November 10, 2002. <http://www.hartford-hwp.com/archives/43a/254.html>.

———. Interview with Wedsly Turenne Guerrier Ph.D. November 2, 2023.

———. *Poetry in Haitian Creole: A guide for beginners and translators*. Soup To Nuts Publishers, 1993.

———. *Sezon sechrès Ayiti: Woman ayisyen*. Soup To Nuts Publishers, 1994.

Weisbrot, Mark. "Haiti and the International Aid Scam." The Guardian (UK), April 22, 2011.

Conclusion

In conclusion, as this book demonstrates, Haiti is a country that has experienced many challenging events. Haitian literature, at different times of Haitian history, has chronicled the impact of various forms of colonization. Chapter 1 shows that colonization, which was the first tragedy experienced by displaced Africans in Saint-Domingue, had a negative impact on future Haitians. In Coicou's poem, the speaker does not like his color because of the trauma associated with Blackness. The self-hatred that he develops might be a reaction to the damage of being enslaved and oppressed. He realizes that because of his Blackness, he becomes a living possession, an instrument of production. He is in a constant state of misery because as a Black person he is tied to slavery and all the burdens that are associated with it. The poem highlights the horrible mental and physical conditions of the slave as well as the sadistic nature of his master. Massillon Coicou's poem *"Complaintes d'Esclave"* shows the trauma associated with slavery as well as the role of religion on slaves' lives. They were forced to believe in God and follow their owners/masters' commands no matter the circumstance. Religion was used as a tool to enslave and manipulate Africans. The slaves were taught that in order to be saved, they were supposed to be obedient and follow to the letter the master's commands. Any type of retaliation was reprimanded with harsh punishments, which do not exclude death.

As Chapter 2 indicated, Aimé Césaire's *Tragedy of King Christophe* underlines that after Emperor Jean-Jacques Dessalines' death in 1806, there were serious debates between Alexandre Pétion and Henry Christophe about the future of this new nation. Tensions rose regarding the type of government that was to be established and how Haiti was to be governed. Building a new nation was not an easy task. Because the two leaders could not settle their issues, Christophe left Port-au-Prince to rule as King in the North and Pétion became President of the west and the south sides of the country. This chapter shows that the character Christophe in Césaires' play utilizes many strategies to gain, exert, and retain power. Christophe had good intentions to develop his kingdom and show Black greatness, but the way he went about doing so was not fair to the population. Even if Christophe and Pétion wanted to protect the new nation and make it prosperous, their approaches to governing differed so much that the country was divided into two. In the end, it was the masses that suffered the consequences.

If divisions among Haitian politicians prevented the country from showing its full capability, the American occupation of Haiti would worsen the situation and caused many Haitian intellectuals to react forcefully against the occupiers. Jacques Roumain was one of those rebel intellectuals who were imprisoned many times for his stances against oppressions. As mentioned in Chapter 3, Roumain used his pen as an instrument to show the ruses used by the Americans to occupy Haiti as well as their human rights violations. He pointed out that the Americans allowed France to take control of education in Haiti and the Catholic Church was used to indoctrinate Haitians. Roumain took a firm stance against the anti-superstition campaign and the negative impact of the Catholic Church on Haitians. To him, the true campaign should have been about alleviating poverty. He stressed that priests spent their time preaching about salvation while the majority of their believers were unemployed, lacked healthcare, needed schools, and social services to improve their lives. He advised his contemporaries to leave behind the gospel of resignation to stand up for their rights as citizens. He believed that the Catholic Church should contribute to the well-being of its community.

After the American occupation of Haiti, the country was more or less stable and attracted many tourists. However, the Duvalier dynasty (1957–1986) changed the country with its dictatorial tendencies. Chapter 4 shows that Anne-Christine d'Adesky's *Under the Bone* highlights the plight of women right after the fall of Baby Doc. She sheds light on the crimes committed by the military that terrorized many women who never found justice. This novel helps the reader understand the pretexts used by the military to cover up their acts. This study helps bring to light many of the difficulties experienced by Haitians, especially women. Using police reports, autopsy results, interviews, newspapers, hospital and prison visits, the narrator compiles evidence to prove the criminalization of ordinary Haitians and activists who were trying to fight injustice, even if she presents it as fiction.

Under the Duvalier regime, many Haitians did not feel safe in Haiti. In order to stay away from the oppressive Duvalier regimes, and in such of job opportunities, many Haitians left the country. While some went to the United States, others ended up in the Dominican Republic. It is fair to say that many of those Haitians had a bad experience in the neighboring country. Chapter 5 demonstrates that Jean-Claude Martineau uses his poem "*Vyewo*" as an instrument to help Haitians reflect critically about migration to the Dominican Republic. While other singers focus on the mistreatment of Haitians by the Dominican government, and their plight in the bateyes, Martineau brings another dimension to the debate by focusing on the psychological impact of father absence on children, wives, and relationships. This poem pays significant homage to women because the wife, who was left with two kids under her care for years, not only did her best to raise them, but remained faithful to her husband. She is actually the one who, after realizing that her husband's trip to the Dominican Republic was a failure, advises him to come back to be with his family and work at home. She makes the husband realize that important events happened in his absence and provides a solid argument for his return.

While Jean-Claude Martineau uses the wise wife to bring the husband to his senses, in Chapter 6, Emmanuel Védrine, in his poem "*Manman pa ban m tet ankò*," utilizes the allegory of a child to repress manipulative authority. In this powerful poem, the child challenges his mother by telling her that for a child his age, breastfeeding is no longer necessary. He needs real food full of vitamins that can make him strong to face life's challenges. He enumerates the foods that he no longer needs and tells her the ones that he would prefer. That poem that seems to be about tensions between a mother and her child can be used to express the sentiment that many Haitians have toward the international community that is treating Haitians as children by imposing decisions on them and telling them how to run their business. Chapter 6 highlights that just like the insolent child, Haitians know what is good for them and challenge the piece-meal solutions proposed by the foreign power to its multiple problems.

This work is significant because it studies some of the less-known, polemical texts regarding Haiti and its people. They offer unique voices that present significant perspectives on Haitian culture. The variety of texts presented in this book shows that when talking about Haitian literature, French is not the only language used by writers. At present, many Haitians live in the Dominican Republic and with the migration of Haitians to Brazil, Chile, Mexico and other Latin American countries, there will be Haitian literature in Spanish, and Portuguese soon. A great number of Haitian writers are producing great works that are going unnoticed. This book attempts to highlight that there are more compelling works about Haiti and its people, not popular in literary circles, that need to be explored.

Notes

[1] In her novel, d'Adesky uses a unique strategy of adapting facts into fiction. During my interview with her, d'Adesky confessed that, while she had documented many events that occurred in Haiti, she didn't feel she could publish in the press everything she had seen. Writing an adapted novel about it proved a better means to bring awareness to the crimes committed in Haiti. She mentions, "These characters are all composites of people that I know. None of them is an actual person, but they are all based on people that I knew a little bit."

Anne-Christine d'Adesky. Interview with Wedsly Turenne Guerrier. Brooklyn. October 6, 2023.

[2] The narrator, Leslie Doyle, is a white human rights activist from Washington DC, who travels to Haiti six months after the uprooting of Jean-Claude Duvalier's regime. Her purpose is to gather the oral histories of the women who have been mistreated while in Haiti's prisons. Leslie represents the white humanitarians coming to Haiti with good intentions but a lack of understanding about what is happening politically. The novel depicts some Haitian women who have suffered at the hands of the Duvalierist regime and are hesitant to share with Leslie, the narrator. They believe that foreigners tend to document their stories but then do nothing afterward to change the situation. Most of the time, these women are punished by prison guards for speaking about their experiences.

Index

Adesky (d'), Anne-Christine 4, 7, 8, 77–89, 134
   Beyond Shock ... 78
   Moving Mountains ... 77
   The Pox Lover ... 78
   The Village Voice 77, 83
   Under the Bone 7, 77, 80–89, 134
Africa 28, 48, 77, 127
AIDS 77, 78
American occupation 6, 7, 39–42, 45, 46, 49, 55, 69, 133, 134
   Admiral Caperton 39
   Borno, Louis 39, 44
   Excise Tax Law 46
   Monroe Doctrine 39
Antilles 26, 115
Aristide, Jean-Bertrand 4, 97

Barthes, Roland 125
batey 103, 107
Beauvoir (de), Simone 82
Black 5, 7, 14, 15, 16, 18, 22, 26, 28, 57, 58, 59, 132
   Black people 20, 35, 60, 65, 66, 68
   Black slave 13, 20
   Blackness 5, 11, 13, 15, 16, 132
   Negritude 27, 68
breastfeeding 9, 115, 120, 121, 124, 135
Breton, André 27, 28
Brown, John 65

capitalism 39, 47, 55
Caribbean 6, 25, 27, 28, 39, 56, 57
Césaire, Aimé 4, 6, 25–36, 132
   L'Étudiant Noir 26
   The Tragedy of King Christophe 6, 25, 28
   Tropiques 27
Charles, Carolle 86
Christian religion 6
   anti-superstition campaign 40, 48, 52, 133
   Bible 5, 13, 21, 57
   Catholic church 6, 40, 42, 49, 50, 51, 55, 63, 69

Catholicism 35, 39, 49, 51, 53
Christ 7, 50, 55, 57–68, 69
God 5, 6, 13–22, 32, 58, 64, 66, 68, 132
gospel of resignation 7, 66, 133
Christophe, Henri 6, 25, 27–36, 132, 133
   Académie Royale 36
   Citadelle 35
   Code Henry 35
   Military Penal Code 35
   Sans Souci palace 35
civil war 13
Clorméus, Lewis A. 53, 73
Coicou, Massillon 4, 5, 11–23, 132
   Amica 12
   Complaintes d'Esclave 5, 13–22
   Impressions 12
   L'Oracle 11
   Les Fils de Toussaint 11
   Passions 12
   Poésies nationales 11, 12
colonialism 6, 13, 28, 40, 57, 79
   colonial legacy 5
   colonial power 9, 125
   colonization 4, 6, 34, 68, 127, 132
communist party 47
Condé, Maryse 89
corruption 7, 77, 84
corvée 46
Coulthard, Gabriel R. 57, 66
crimes 7, 134

Dash, Michael 39
Death 5, 13, 14
dechoukaj movement 83
decolonization 34
democracy 4, 39, 40, 52
despots 31
Dessalines, Jean-Jacques 6, 25, 35, 132
Destin, Yven 35
dictatorship 5, 81, 97
Dominican Republic 8, 45, 102, 103, 105, 107, 109, 120, 134, 135
Dominique, Jean 99, 100
Dorsinville, Roger 46

INDEX

Dubossy, Marie-Thérèse 86, 87
Duvalier 7, 8, 80, 81, 83, 84, 85, 87, 89, 101, 117, 134
    Duvalier dictatorships 4, 8, 79, 98
    Fort Dimanche 83, 102
    Lucerne, Henri 87
    Titanyen 83, 102
    Tontons Macoutes 81, 84, 88, 102

earthquake 78, 126
exploitation 22, 52, 59, 65, 89
expropriations 45

Fanon, Frantz 11, 56, 115, 125
    Black Skin, White Masks 11
    The Wretched of the Earth 56, 125
Ferguson, James 102
Fils-Aimé, Jean 34, 36
Fonkoua, Romuald 26
Foudou, Jean Numa 96
Fowler, Caroline 41
France 12, 26, 29, 31, 35, 55, 80, 127, 133
freedom 8, 9, 16, 17, 18, 19, 22, 31, 33, 34, 53, 54, 96, 125

gagaire 28
Gaillard, Roger 43
Gouraige, Ghislain 13

Haiti 4, 6, 7, 9, 31, 34, 35, 40, 45, 52, 62, 69, 77, 80, 81, 82, 83, 86, 88, 95, 97, 99, 102, 109, 116–20, 125–28
    African culture 40, 68
    Civil War 29
    Eurocentric model 49
    Haitian culture 42, 55, 56, 95–102, 106, 135
    Haitian diaspora 96, 97, 99, 119, 127
    Haitian identity 6, 40, 41, 42, 95
    Haitian literature 5, 15, 43, 132, 135
    Haitian migration 8, 101, 109, 134, 135
    Haitian Revolution 4
    Haitian women 7, 8, 79, 80, 85, 88
    paradise 32, 34, 116
    Port-au-Prince 13, 25, 45, 96, 133
Harris, Rodney E. 34

Holden, Sue 78
human rights 7, 33, 82–87, 133

imperialism 13, 47
independence 9, 12, 27, 31, 32, 34, 115, 125
Indigenist movement 12
international community 4, 86, 87, 126, 128, 135

Jean, Eddy Arnold 12, 46, 67
Jernegan, Marcus W. 56
Jesus *Voir* Christ
Joseph, Celucien L. 41, 52, 53, 55

kongo 103

L'Ouverture, Toussaint 27
Laraque, Franck 64, 68
Le Pen, Jean-Marie 79
Leconte, Frantz-Antoine 43, 48, 68
Legros Georges, Danielle 98, 99
Les deux Magots 82
Lescot, Élie 48, 56
Linguistics 4, 116, 117
    English 5, 8, 57, 80, 85, 89, 101, 116, 117
    French 4, 5, 14, 25, 80, 85, 95, 97, 101, 116, 119, 135
    Haitian Creole 4, 5, 8, 9, 85, 96, 97, 101, 102, 103, 106, 109, 115, 116–19
    Portuguese 5, 135
    Spanish 5, 85, 116, 135
Louis, Martine 13, 26, 39, 118
Luczama, Statler 96

Maguire, Robert 98
Makouta-Mboukou, Jean-Pierre 45, 50
Maribaroux Plain 127
Martineau, Jean-Claude 4, 8, 9, 100, 101, 95–109, 119, 134, 135
    Ayiti Demen 97, 98
    Flè Dizè: Powèm chante 95, 101
    Haïti Culturelle 96, 97
    Vyewo 8, 95, 97, 101–9, 134
Martinique 26, 27
Ménard, Nadève 103
Michel, Claudine 78

INDEX

Michel, Jean-Claude 43
MINUSTAH 9, 125
misery 16, 19, 21, 22, 52, 62, 64, 132
Moreau, Alain 32, 33
Morisseau-Leroy, Félix 96
mulattoes 25, 29, 30

Nzengou-Tayo, Marie-José 42

peace 13, 39, 66
peasants 13, 32, 42, 44, 45, 46, 47, 49, 50, 51, 53, 69, 89, 95, 120, 127
people of Haiti *See* Haitians
Pétion, Alexandre 6, 25, 28, 29, 30, 31, 34, 132, 133
Pierre Nord, Alexis 12
Poetics 4
political oppression 8, 80, 88
Postcolonialism 4
power 5, 6, 9, 13, 22, 25, 29, 30, 31, 32, 33, 39, 58, 59, 62, 67, 68, 70, 85, 125, 128, 133, 135
Price Mars, Jean 12, 42
  So Spoke the Uncle 42

racism 11, 21, 28
resistance 5, 9, 31, 41, 69, 89
Roberts, Shearon 126
Roumain, Jacques 4, 6, 7, 42, 39–70, 133
  A propos de la campagne anti-supersticieuse 50
  Analyse schématique 43, 46
  Autour de la taxe … 43
  Bois d'ébène 56
  Brouard, Carl 42
  Heurtelou, Daniel 42
  La Revue Indigène 42
  Nouveau Sermon Nègre 7, 56–69
  Réplique finale au Réverend Père Foisset 50
Roumer, Emile 42

Sylvain, Normil 42
Thoby-Marcelin, Philippe 42
Vieux, Antonio 42
Roumain, Marika 95

Saint-Domingue 4, 132
Schulman, Sarah 79
slavery 4, 5, 6, 13, 15, 16, 21, 22, 25, 33, 60, 68, 70, 132
  abolishment 34, 35
  bondage 17, 18, 58, 62
  Code Noir 56
Sylvain, Georges 42

terror 7, 64, 65, 70, 84
Thadal, Marc Roland 43, 68
Toussaint, Hérold 45, 48, 55
Trouillot, Henock 47, 68

United States 4, 8, 25, 35, 39, 45, 55, 87, 96, 97, 116, 119, 134
United States Occupation *See* American Occupation

Valdmann, Albert 115
Védrine, Emmanuel 4, 9, 115–28, 135
  E. W. Védrine Creole Project 119
  Manman, pa banm tete ankò 9, 115, 120–27
  Sezon sechrès Ayiti: Woman ayisy 120
Voodoo 7, 40, 48, 49, 50, 55, 69
  loas 32, 51, 53
  Papa Legba 32

white 15
  whiteness 11
Williams, Fred 97
Wilson, Victor-Emmanuel Roberto 35

Zeleza, Paul Tiyambe 86

Tamara Alvarez-Detrell and Michael G. Paulson
General Editors

Caribbean Studies treats all aspects of Caribbean culture and society, including, but not necessarily limited to, literatures, history, film, music, art, geography, politics, languages, and social sciences. Studies may focus on European, Amerindian, African, or Asian heritages or on a combination of any/all of the above. Linear and chronological approaches, as well as comparative studies are welcome. Places and/or cultures under study may include English-, Spanish-, French-, or Dutch-speaking areas in any time frame or discipline. Manuscripts may be written in English, Spanish, or French, preferably in the language in which the author feels most comfortable. Studies may be on contemporary or previous periods and, if appropriate, can draw comparisons with other global regions.

For additional information about the series or for the submission of manuscripts, please contact:

>Acquisitions Department
>c/o Peter Lang Publishing, Inc.
>80 Broad Street, 5th floor
>New York, NY 10004

To order other books in this series, please contact our Customer Service Department:

>peterlang@presswarehouse.com (within the U.S.)
>order@peterlang.com (outside the U.S.)

Or browse online by series at:

>www.peterlang.com

www.ingramcontent.com/pod-product-compliance
Lightning Source LLC
Chambersburg PA
CBHW061719300426
44115CB00014B/2755